T0148507

THE BEEF

THE BEEF

A Historical View of Great Hitting Combos during the "Age of Pitching" in Major League Baseball in the 1960s

HARRY LOCKHART JR

authorHOUSE®

AuthorHouse™
1663 Liberty Drive
Bloomington, IN 47403
www.authorhouse.com
Phone: 1-800-839-8640

authorHOUSE®

© *2013 Harry Lockhart Jr. All rights reserved.*

No part of this book may be reproduced, stored in a retrieval system, or transmitted by any means without the written permission of the author.

Published by AuthorHouse 2/19/2013

ISBN: 978-1-4817-1324-5 (sc)
ISBN: 978-1-4817-1325-2 (hc)
ISBN: 978-1-4817-1326-9 (e)

Library of Congress Control Number: 2013902456

Topps baseball cards used courtesy of The Topps Company, Inc. For more information about The Topps Company, please see our website at www.topps.com.

Any people depicted in stock imagery provided by Thinkstock are models, and such images are being used for illustrative purposes only. Certain stock imagery © Thinkstock.

This book is printed on acid-free paper.

Because of the dynamic nature of the Internet, any web addresses or links contained in this book may have changed since publication and may no longer be valid. The views expressed in this work are solely those of the author and do not necessarily reflect the views of the publisher, and the publisher hereby disclaims any responsibility for them.

In the heat of the pennant race on 8-22-1965, veteran home plate umpire Shag Crawford (right) attempted to stop San Francisco's Juan Marichal's bat assault on Dodger catcher John Roseboro. (see cover). He eventually found himself at the bottom of the pile of this famous brawl. The legendary Crawford served 20 years as an NL umpire in over 3100 games from 1956-1975.

Pictured to his left is his son, former NL MLB umpire Jerry Crawford. Jerry followed in his famous father's footsteps and retired in 2010 after 34 years of a potential hall of fame career himself.

1960 MLB Final Standings

National League			American League		
Team	Record	Gm Bk	Team	Record	Gm Bk
Pittsburgh Pirates	95–59	—	New York Yankees	97–57	—
Milwaukee Braves	88–66	7	Baltimore Orioles	89–65	8
St Louis Cardinals	86–68	9	Chicago White Sox	87–67	10
Los Angeles Dodgers	82–72	13	Cleveland Indians	76–78	21
San Francisco Giants	79–75	16	Washington Senators	73–81	24
Cincinnati Reds	67–87	28	Detroit Tigers	71–83	26
Chicago Cubs	60–94	35	Boston Red Sox	65–89	32
Philadelphia Phillies	59–95	36	Kansas City Athletics	58–96	39

1961 MLB Final Standings

National League			American League		
Team	Record	Gm Bk	Team	Record	Gm Bk
Cincinnati Reds	93–61	—	New York Yankees	109–53	—
Los Angeles Dodgers	89–65	4	Detroit Tigers	101–61	8
San Francisco Giants	85–69	8	Baltimore Orioles	95–67	14
Milwaukee Braves	83–71	10	Chicago White Sox	86–76	23
St Louis Cardinals	80–74	13	Cleveland Indians	78–83	30.5

Pittsburgh Pirates	75–79	18	Boston Red Sox	76–86	33
Chicago Cubs	64–90	29	Minnesota Twins	70–90	38
Philadelphia Phillies	47–107	46	Los Angeles Angels	70–91	38.5
			Washington Senators	61–100	47.5
			Kansas City Athletics	61–100	47.5

1962 MLB FINAL STANDINGS

National League			American League		
Team	Record	Gm Bk	Team	Record	Gm Bk
San Francisco Giants *	103–62	—	New York Yankees	96–66	—
Los Angeles Dodgers*	102–63	1	Minnesota Twins	91–71	5
Cincinnati Reds	98–64	3.5	Los Angeles Angels	86–76	10
Pittsburgh Pirates	93–68	8	Detroit Tigers	85–76	10.5
Milwaukee Braves	86–76	15.5	Chicago White Sox	85–77	11
St Louis Cardinals	84–78	17.5	Cleveland Indians	80–82	16
Philadelphia Phillies	81–80	20	Baltimore Orioles	77–85	19
Houston Colt45s	64–96	36.5	Boston Red Sox	76–84	20
Chicago Cubs	59–103	42.5	Kansas City Athletics	72–90	24
New York Mets	40–120	60.5	Washington Senators	60–101	35.5

*Record includes 3 game regular season playoff won by the Giants 2 games to one.

1963 MLB Final Standings

National League			American League		
Team	Record	Gm Bk	Team	Record	Gm Bk
Los Angeles Dodgers	99–63	—	New York Yankees	104–57	—
St Louis Cardinals	93–69	6	Chicago White Sox	94–68	10.5
San Francisco Giants	88–74	11	Minnesota Twins	91–70	13
Philadelphia Phillies	87–75	12	Baltimore Orioles	86–76	18.5
Cincinnati Reds	86–76	13	Cleveland Indians	79–83	25.5
Milwaukee Braves	84–78	15	Detroit Tigers	79–83	25.5
Chicago Cubs	82–80	17	Boston Red Sox	76–85	28
Pittsburgh Pirates	74–88	25	Kansas City Athletics	73–89	31.5
Houston Colt 45s	66–96	33	Los Angeles Angels	70–91	34
New York Mets	51–111	48	Washington Senators	56–106	48.5

1964 MLB Final Standings

National League			American League		
Team	Record	Gm Bk	Team	Record	Gm Bk
St Louis Cardinals	93–69	—	New York Yankees	99–63	—
Cincinnati Reds	92–70	1	Chicago White Sox	98–64	1
Philadelphia Phillies	92–70	1	Baltimore Orioles	97–65	2

San Francisco Giants	90–72	3	Detroit Tigers	85–77	14
Milwaukee Braves	88–74	5	Los Angeles Angels	82–80	17
Los Angeles Dodgers	80–82	13	Cleveland Indians	79–83	20
Pittsburgh Pirates	80–82	13	Minnesota Twins	79–83	20
Chicago Cubs	76–86	17	Boston Red Sox	72–90	27
Houston Colt 45s	66–96	27	Washington Senators	62–100	37
New York Mets	53–109	40	Kansas City Athletics	57–105	42

1965 MLB FINAL STANDINGS

National League			American League		
Team	Record	Gm Bk	Team	Record	Gm Bk
Los Angeles Dodgers	97–65	—	Minnesota Twins	102–60	—
San Francisco Giants	95–67	2	Chicago White Sox	95–67	7
Pittsburgh Pirates	90–72	7	Baltimore Orioles	94–68	8
Cincinnati Reds	89–73	8	Detroit Tigers	89–73	13
Milwaukee Braves	86–76	11	Cleveland Indians	87–75	15
Philadelphia Phillies	85–76	11.5	New York Yankees	77–85	25
St Louis Cardinals	80–81	16.5	California Angels	75–87	27
Chicago Cubs	72–90	25	Washington Senators	70–92	32

Houston Astros	65–97	32	Boston Red Sox	62–100	40
New York Mets	50–112	47	Kansas City Athletics	59–103	43

1966 MLB FINAL STANDINGS

National League			American League		
Team	Record	Gm Bk	Team	Record	Gm Bk
Los Angeles Dodgers	95–67	—	Baltimore Orioles	97–63	—
San Francisco Giants	93–68	1.5	Minnesota Twins	89–73	9
Pittsburgh Pirates	92–70	3	Detroit Tigers	88–74	10
Philadelphia Phillies	87–75	8	Chicago White Sox	83–79	15
Atlanta Braves	85–77	10\	Cleveland Indians	81–81	17
St Louis Cardinals	83–79	12	California Angeles	80–82	18
Cincinnati Reds	76–84	18	Kansas City Athletics	74–86	23
Houston Astros	72–90	23	Washington Senators	71–88	25.5
New York Mets	66–95	28.5	Boston Red Sox	72–90	26
Chicago Cubs	59–103	36	New York Yankees	70–89	26.5

1967 MLB Final Standings

National League			American League		
Team	Record	Gm Bk	Team	Record	Gm Bk
St Louis Cardinals	101–60	—	Boston Red Sox	92–70	—
San Francisco Giants	91–71	10.5	Detroit Tigers	91–71	1
Chicago Cubs	87–74	14	Minnesota Twins	91–71	1
Cincinnati Reds	87–74	14.5	Chicago White Sox	89–73	3
Philadelphia Phillies	82–80	19.5	California Angeles	84–77	7.5
Pittsburgh Pirates	81–81	20.5	Baltimore Orioles	76–85	15.5
Atlanta Braves	77–85	24.5	Washington Senators	76–85	15.5
Los Angeles Dodgers	73–89	28.5	Cleveland Indians	75–87	17
Houston Astros	69–93	32.5	New York Yankees	72–90	20
New York Mets	61–101	40.5	Kansas City Athletics	62–99	29.5

1968 MLB Final Standings

National League			American League		
Team	Record	Gm Bk	Team	Record	Gm Bk
St Louis Cardinals	97–65	—	Detroit Tigers	103–59	—
San Francisco Giants	88–74	9	Baltimore Orioles	91–71	12
Chicago Cubs	84–78	13	Cleveland Indians	86–75	16.5

Team	Record	Gm Bk	Team	Record	Gm Bk
Cincinnati Reds	83–79	14	Boston Red Sox	86–76	17
Atlanta Braves	81–81	16	New York Yankees	83–79	20
Pittsburgh Pirates	80–82	17	Oakland Athletics	82–80	21
Los Angeles Dodgers	76–86	21	Minnesota Twins	79–83	24
Philadelphia Phillies	76–86	21	California Angels	67–95	36
New York Mets	73–89	24	Chicago White Sox	67–95	36
Houston Astros	72–94	25	Washington Senators	65–96	37.5

1969 MLB FINAL STANDINGS

National League			American League		
EAST DIVISION					
Team	Record	Gm Bk	Team	Record	Gm Bk
New York Mets	100–62	—	Baltimore Orioles	109–53	—
Chicago Cubs	92–70	8	Detroit Tigers	90–72	19
Pittsburgh Pirates	88–74	12	Boston Red Sox	87–75	22
St Louis Cardinals	87–75	13	Washington Senators	86–76	23
Philadelphia Phillies	63–99	37	New York Yankees	80–81	28.5
Montreal Expos	52–110	48	Cleveland Indians	62–99	46.5
WEST DIVISION					
Atlanta Braves	93–69	—	Minnesota Twins	97–65	—

San Francisco Giants	90–72	3	Oakland Athletics	88–74	9
Cincinnati Reds	89–73	4	California Angels	71–91	26
Los Angeles Dodgers	85–77	8	Kansas City Royals	69–93	28
Houston Astros	81–81	12	Chicago White Sox	68–94	29
San Diego Padres	52–110	41	Seattle Pilots	64–98	33

TABLE OF CONTENTS

INTRODUCTION

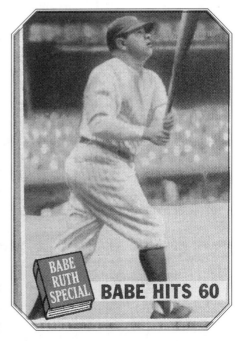

BABE HITS 60

Since the days of Babe Ruth, Lou Gehrig, and Murderer's Row in the 1920s, major league teams have been trying to get "the beef" into the middle of their lineups to excite fans with eye-popping power in an attempt to earn big profits through a dedicated fan base that creates high attendance at the stadium.

The fans have responded by showing up at ballparks across the country to see these great hitting combinations. In the 1960s, there were many great combinations like Maris and Mantle, Mays and McCovey, and Mathews and Aaron. So impressive were these combos that fans still rave about them, even today. However, most recently fans loved to watch Mark McGwire and Jose Canseco,

Manny Ramirez and David Ortiz, or Matt Holiday and Albert Pujols—the millionaires of swat. Americans love power and home runs in their lineups. In fact the long ball and home run highlights are to ESPN what the German Third Reich is to the Military Channel; people turn on and tune in to these channels to for those purposes alone. However, with all the emphasis over the last hundred years on creating the beef in the middle of the lineup, how important has it been for teams that had those power combos in the middle of their lineups?

My goal is to answer the following questions as they relate to each team of the 1960s with a detailed look and an emphasis on their lineup and so-called meat, the 3-4-5 spots of the batting order.

1. What teams had the best 3-4-5 hitting combinations?

2. How did each of these team's combinations contribute to championships?

3. Did the great combos live up to their potential?

4. Were there other factors that led to their team's success and failures?

5. Who were the best teams of the 1960s, and why?

6. Who were the worst teams of the decade, and why?

7. Which was the better league, the National or American?

8. In an age dominated by pitching, how did the hitters survive?

9. What franchises overachieved, which underachieved, and why?

10. Who were the unusual characters that played an important role during the decade, and what did their contributions bring to the era?

THE DECADE OF THE 1960s

The decade of the 1960s was indeed a tribute to time. Outside of the baseball world, the era started with the end of the conservative 1950s Eisenhower reign, with the election of John Kennedy. Kennedy brought a flair of adventure, change, and excitement to the country. During this time, there were national threats, assassinations of our leaders, violence in our major cities, racial issues, a war, and a decade that would end in dramatic fashion by placing a man on the moon. Major League Baseball was no different in its own challenges and problems.

In 1960, baseball ushered in the perennial AL champs from the 1950s, the New York Yankees. In dramatic fashion, they would lose the 1960 World Series to the underdog Pittsburgh Pirates. By the end of the decade, the other New York team, baseball's worst, would land their man on the moon, as the New York Mets would be the world champions of 1969. The decade would claim the lives and cut short the careers of some of its upcoming stars; there would be racial tension and issues. By the end of the '60s, one of MLB's stars would sacrifice a potential Hall of Fame career over the color of his skin in opposition to "baseball slavery" and the reserve clause. There would be wars and threats over players' rights off the field. There would be wars on the field, including the winningest pitcher of the decade, Juan Marichal, using his bat to hit the head of prominent Dodger catcher John Roseboro in the middle of a heated pennant race. (see cover) Inside the baseball world was the reflection of the issues and challenges of the outside world.

GREATEST INVENTION KNOWN TO MAN

Like so many kids at the time, I lived this period of my life every night in bed, listening to my transistor radio. I had it carefully tucked under my pillow on low volume, so as to not get caught staying up late and following my heroes. With my imagination, I could see every play clearly until I eventually dozed off to sleep.

Although it may have not been the greatest invention known to man, the transistor radio was the finest thing ever invented for the kids of the 1950s and 1960s. It first started to be mass marketed in 1954. Although it was very limited to a few AM stations, with poor reception, this predecessor of the boom box was a must-have for all young baseball fans. It weighed less than eight ounces and fit nicely into the front shirt pocket. By the time I was eight years old, transistors were in full swing and could be bought for under fifteen dollars. It was an automatic for the Christmas list.

It was through this invention that the magical voices of Bob Prince, Ernie Harwell, Harry Caray, Vince Scully, and others were able to bring the baseball icons to audiences day after day. Regardless of where you were, the transistor was portable, and you could listen to the game if you were at the store, in the car, at the beach, in bed, or even at school. (Oops! Did I say that last one?) The biggest obstacle was the battery: if it was dead, so were you. If you were lucky enough to have an extra, and a friend's went dead, you were in fat city! By the end of the day, you probably had all his Mickey Mantle baseball cards in order to get him up and working. If he wasn't a friend, you had his Stan Musial cards, too! And if he was someone you really hated, you had his entire collection, plus a date with his sister. It was by this simple supply-and-demand process of the battery that I was able to understand widgets and economic theory later in life.

"I watched a lot of baseball on the radio."
—Gerald Ford, baseball fan and US president

THE HITTERS OF THE 1960s

"He hits from both sides of the plate. He's amphibious!"
—Yogi Berra

During the 1960s the 3-4 hitting combinations rate as some of the greatest in baseball history. Even some of the teams that consistently finished in the second division had wonderful middle-of-the-order hitters. There were some teams that boasted not only a great 3-4 combo but also had outstanding hitters and sometimes Hall of Famers in

the fifth spot. The Giants from 1960–1966 had Willie Mays, Willie McCovey, and Orlando Cepeda. The Cubs throughout most of the decade featured Billy Williams, Ron Santo, and Ernie Banks. In both these cases, all three spots were represented by future Hall of Famers. Right up there with these phenomenal lineups were the Yankees, with Roger Maris, Mickey Mantle, and Yogi Berra. The early 1960s Milwaukee Braves had Hank Aaron, Ed Mathews, and Joe Adcock in their 3-4-5 spots, which had produced pennants in 1957 and again in 1958. The 1961–1963 Detroit Tigers had an awesome combination of Al Kaline, Norm Cash, and Rocky Colavito. The Orioles of the last half of the 1960s had the middle occupied by Frank Robinson, Boog Powell, and Brooks Robinson, which led to several championships. In addition, other clubs who did not have all three spots as powerful still had fantastic 3-4 combinations of their own. This group included the Pirates' hitting machines of Roberto Clemente and Willie Stargell. The Phillies' Johnny Callison and Richie Allen had several great years, and the Reds' combo of Vada Pinson and Frank Robinson won the 1961 NL pennant. The Minnesota Twins' 3-4 spots were ruled by Tony Oliva and Harmon Killebrew, while New England enjoyed "Tony C" and "Yaz." Nonetheless, none of the clubs here suffered a power shortage. Several of these combinations yielded in excess of a thousand homers for their clubs during the 1960s—the beef was everywhere! How could

pitching staffs of the decade survive these numerous, once-in-a-lifetime batting combinations?

The Pitchers of the 1960s

"Good pitching will always stop good hitting, and vice versa."
—Casey Stengel

The 1960s has been referred to as the golden age of pitching. There were outstanding stars and Hall of Famers who continued their pitching careers from the 1950s; Warren Spahn, Whitey Ford, Robin Roberts, Hoyt Wilhelm, Jim Bunning, and Early Wynn were among this group. There were others who blossomed during the decade; this group consisted of Sandy Koufax, Bob Gibson, Juan Marichal, Don Drysdale, Gaylord Perry, Ferguson Jenkins, Jim Palmer, Tom Seaver, Denny McClain, Jim Kaat, Phil Niekro, and Dave McNally, most of who have plaques in Cooperstown. There were several who began their careers in the '60s who would have a bigger impact in the next decade: Steve Carlton, Nolan Ryan, Catfish Hunter, Rollie Fingers, Don Sutton, and Luis Tiant; several of these went on to be Hall of Famers .Then there were other outstanding pitchers who were simply overmatched by comparison to this outstanding group, yet they were very talented; these were the Jim Maloneys, the Stan Williams, the Mike Cuellars, the Walley Bunkers, the Camillio Pasquals, the Joey Jays, the Wilbur Woods, and the Bob Veales. All were outstanding pitchers in their careers, but they were placed wrongly in baseball history for recognition of their talents and accomplishments.

In 1961 Whitey Ford was 25–4, for a .862 winning percentage. Sandy Koufax pitched no-hitters in 1962, 1963, and 1964, and a perfect game in 1965, while leading the league in ERA five consecutive years. In 1967 Bob Gibson finished the year with an ERA of 1.12, and in 1968, Don Drysdale would pitch a record fifty-six straight scoreless innings. These were just a sampling of this group's achievements.

In retrospect, the pitchers of the 1960s may have been the largest abundance of talented hurlers ever in the game. However, with all this pitching talent, how truly great were these hitters during this period? How much beef did the middle of the lineup need to offset this barrage of pitching greats? Was it even possible to do so?

In the so-called age of pitching, Roger Maris broke Babe Ruth's single-season home run record with 61 round trippers in 1961. The Yankees set a team home run record with a total of 240 in a season in 1961, and Willie Mays hit 52 home runs in 1965 to become the only person to hit 50-plus home runs ten years apart in a career. Was it the age of pitching, or was it the age of hitting?

BEEF-O-METER

"Hitting the ball was easy. Running around the bases was the tough part." —Mickey Mantle

In 1984, the Wendy's Hamburger Corporation introduced a series of television commercials featuring an eighty-two-year-old Jewish manicurist from Chicago. Her name was Clara Pellar. In the famous commercials, Pellar continuously shouts out in the competition's fast food restaurant's lobby, asking, "Where's the beef?" She was referring to her hamburger. The commercials soon became iconic, and Pellar was a star. Wendy's got the beef in the form of huge profits from the recognition of the ads. Even today, the words are often shouted out in a comical way by many Americans in party situations.

How do we determine where the "beef" was, and how much "beef" did each team have? We will be taking a detailed look at the batting orders of each of the teams of the 1960s. We will concentrate not only on the three and four slots; but the entire middle of the order, which would also include the number five spot. Because most teams rarely kept the same lineup for a substantial number of consecutive years, we'll divide the period into two parts: the first time frame will be 1960–1964, and the second will be from 1965–1969. The most frequently used lineup for each period will be placed on our Beef-O-Meter.

Teams can earn up to a total of ten points during each period measured.

They will be scored by the following rules. Teams will be given three points for most Hall of Famers (the exception being if they were on the decline—i.e., Stan Musial, 1960—1963—or if they were more noted for their defensive skills—i.e., Brooks Robinson). Next, a team can earn two points for a legitimate star that isn't a Hall of Famer. Finally, a team will be awarded one point for a regular who might fit in the category of a minor or semi star. Sometimes when there is no one consistently in the that position, or the player hitting in that spot has below-average numbers, no point will be given.

Teams can further earn an additional point by having the depth of a quality player who can occasionally fill in for one of the other players in the middle of the order. That fill-in player might normally bat somewhere else in the lineup on a regular basis, or he might even be a platoon player.

To illustrate how the Beef-O-Meter might work, let's look at the San Francisco Giants of the early 1960s. Their consistent 3-4-5 hitters included Hall of Famer Willie Mays (three points), Hall of Famer Willie McCovey (three points), and Hall of Famer Orlando Cepeda (three points), for a total of nine points. With substitution help in the 3-4-5 spot from a semi star like Felipe Alou, the Giants pick up another point and earn a total of ten points on our Beef-O-Meter for the period of 1960–1964.

Although the goal is to get an insight into the middle of the orders, I must admit that our Beef-O-Meter is not an exact science and can be subjective to a point. Nonetheless, it does have merit in helping determine several things. One thing is that it gives us a basis to compare one team to another, or the same team from one period during the decade to another. Even if someone else was to evaluate the same players in those same lineups, it would be hard to argue that the overall score would be greatly different. The illustration with the Giants would be a good example. If one person did not award an extra point for Alou, it still would be hard to give the team a score of less than nine. During 1960–1964, Mays hit 203 home runs, Cepeda hit 170, and McCovey hit 113 (losing time to injuries). Even if someone decided to rate McCovey a two and not give the full three points, that same person might feel that Alou would merit an extra point, and we still would wind up with a total score of nine.

Another feature of the Beef-O-Meter is to see how consistent the lineups were during the time. My research consistently points out that the teams that had the same 3-4-5 hitters usually had more success (although the Cubs were one of the few examples of the consistency not matching the winning). What really jumps out in my research is the number of times a team fielded the same one-through-eight hitters(excluding the ninth spot, because pitchers don't hit every day), and how that relates to winning. We will show several examples of teams that, when they began to win, started going with the same full lineup more and more. This makes sense because if a team's 3-4-5 or the full line up is working, why would the manager change it, except for an injury?

Through the Beef-O-Meter, we are able to see the chaos some of the teams had. When fifteen different players are hitting third, fourteen different are hitting fourth, and another twelve are hitting in the fifth spot, the results become pretty predictable. The reason for this is that usually the talent is not there, and the manager is attempting every lineup possibility to create production.

Furthermore, sometimes the Beef-O-Meter points us in a different direction from the heart of the lineup. The Dodgers of the 1960s are a good example of consistently having a low Beef-O-Meter score, but they still churned out championships. When this happens, it leads us to question just how important beef is, anyway. What other factors did they have? Were these other factors even more important than what meets the eye? Certainly the Dodger pitchers were a bigger factor than what might be assumed, but the performance and contributions of Maury Wills and his importance to the Dodgers during the decade now becomes even more noticeable. Similarly, the St. Louis Cardinals had an average middle of the lineup in 1967 and again in 1968, when they won two pennants. Nonetheless, they did score a lot of runs as a result of Lou Brock and Curt Flood, who were at the top of the lineup and really overshadowed the Birds' beef.

Rather than get hung up on the exactness of the Beef-O-Meter, I suggest you enjoy it for what it is. It is a tool to examine whether a team was outstanding, average, or poor in the middle of its lineup. Relive some of great combos in baseball at the time.

So which is it, pitching or power that wins out? It is often said that good pitching beats good hitting. Did those powerhouses that we mention earlier produce pennants and championships, or were they quieted by the great pitching staffs of the decade? Is it all about the beef, or is it something else? See if the teams really did get bang for their bucks as they traded for and paid top dollars to create some of these memorable batting beefs.

Let's start with the National League.

NATIONAL LEAGUE REGULAR SEASON WINS FOR THE 1960s DECADE

San Francisco Giants.....902
St Louis Cardinals........884
Los Angeles Dodgers......878
Cincinnati Reds..............860
Milwaukee/Atlanta Braves..853
Pittsburgh Pirates.............848
Philadelphia Phillies.........759
Chicago Cubs..................731
Houston 45s/Astros.........555 [8 seasons]
New York Mets................494 [8 seasons]

INTRODUCTION TO THE NATIONAL LEAGUE

IT WAS A LEAGUE THAT had as many stars as a clear summer night. There were Willie Mays, Hank Aaron, Roberto Clemente, Stan "The Man" Musial, and a host of other Hall of Famers who continued there NL careers into the sixties. This was the league that would dominate the All Star Games each year, winning twelve of the thirteen games played (in 1960–1962, two All Star games were played each year. This was the league that won six of the ten world championships during the decade.

Not only did the league have great hitting, but it had great pitching as well. There were Sandy Koufax, Don Drysdale, Bob Gibson, Fergie Jenkins, Tom Seaver, and Juan Marichal. All were destined to put their stamp on a Cooperstown career.

The dominant teams were the Los Angeles Dodgers, who won three pennants and two world championships, and the Saint Louis Cardinals, who also won three pennants and two world championships. The winningest team in the regular season would be the San Francisco Giants, with some 902 victories during the decade. Despite averaging slightly more than 90 wins per year, the Giants would have only one pennant to show for their efforts; that lone pennant came as a result of a victory in a three-game playoff of the regular season in 1962, against the Dodgers.

Newcomers to the eight-team league included the Houston Colt 45s and the New York Mets in 1962. Expansion in 1969 added the San Diego Padres and the first MLB team outside American borders, in the form of the Montreal Expos. The latter expansion divided the league into the East and West Divisions and would result in a NL Championship Series to determine who would win the NL pennant and go to the World Series.

DYNAMIC DUOS OF THE NATIONAL LEAGUE

The 1960s were an incredible time for dynamic duos in the third and fourth spot of the batting order. The Braves had Eddie Mathews and Hank Aaron. The Giants had Willie Mays and Willie McCovey. The Phillies had Johnny Callison and Richie Allen. The Cardinals had Bill White and Ken Boyer. The Pirates had Roberto Clemente and Willie Stargell. The Cubbies had Billy Williams and Ron Santo (Santo could have been fifth and Ernie Banks fourth, if they had wanted), and the Reds had Vada Pinson and Frank Robinson. The other teams, although not as prolific, were the Astros with Rusty Staub and Jim Wynn, the Dodgers with Willie Davis and Tommie Davis, and the Mets with ... well, they just had just pitching.

It is little wonder that the National League was so dominant in the All Star and World Series games during the decade. It truly was a great time to watch the national pastime.

ROOKIES OF THE NATIONAL LEAGUE

The influx of great rookies in the National League during the 1960s would be hard to surpass by any other decade in history. Here is a partial list of many of better players making their debut during the decade.

San Francisco Giants: Matty Alou, Juan Marichal, Gaylord Perry, Jim Ray Hart, Manny Mota, Bobby Bonds

Chicago Cubs: Lou Brock, Ron Santo, Billy Williams, Ken Hubbs, Ken Holtzman

St Louis Cardinals: Steve Carlton, Tim McCarver

Milwaukee/Atlanta Braves: Joe Torre, Phil Niekro, Rico Carty, Bob Uecker, Bobby Cox

Philadelphia Phillies: Richie Allen, Ferguson Jenkins

Pittsburgh Pirates: Donn Clendenon, Willie Stargell, Al Oliver, Richie Hebner

Houston Astros: Joe Morgan, Rusty Staub, Jim Wynn, Bob Watson

Cincinnati Reds: Johnny Bench, Pete Rose, Lee May, Tony Perez, Jim Maloney, Tommy Harper, Alex Johnson, Gordy Coleman

New York Mets: Tom Seaver, Nolan Ryan, Tug McGraw, Cleon Jones, Ed Kranepool

Los Angeles Dodgers: Willie Davis, Tommy Davis, Don Sutton, Bill Singer, Ron Fairly, Frank Howard

With so many great players already in the game, this influx of new stars made many outstanding ballplayers Cooperstown questionables by comparison, despite how really talented they were. On the other hand, it made the National League of the 1960s a magical time, with stars everywhere.

SPEED AND THE TOP OF THE LINEUP

As we reviewed the Beef-O-Meter of each team in the National League during the time frame, it quickly becomes apparent that the teams that had outstanding middles were great to go see—but had very little success in winning championships. So true to this pattern were the Cubs' three Hall of Famers—Williams, Santo, and Banks—who combined for nearly 1,300 home runs during their careers, yet the team spent most of the decade near the cellar of the league.

The teams with little hitting but great pitching, like the Mets and the Dodgers, seemed to manufacture runs through speed and protect the leads through defense. The Cardinals, with good pitching and great speed, also reflected this pattern by winning three pennants. In the final analysis, in a decade that pitching results forced the mound to be lowered to help the hitters, championships seemed to be most influenced by the top of the order rather the middle. It was the middle of the order that was for show, whereas the top was for "Go, go, go!" and the dough!

Los Angeles Dodgers

O N FEBRUARY 23, 1960, THE final pain fell over Brooklyn skies as a huge wrecking ball began its demolition of the famed Ebbets Field. Although their beloved Dodgers had last played there on September 24, 1957, it was the final, painful blow to the community that had so dearly embraced them.

From east to west, no franchise went through more transitions than the Dodgers in the late 1950s and the 1960s. This was a team that, in the 1950s, was a beloved neighborhood team in Brooklyn. It played in a small, iconic ballpark called Ebbets Field, the players lived next door to you, and you would see walking around town. This was a team that had won pennants in 1952, 1953, 1955, and 1956. The Dodgers had hitting superstars who answered to the names of Duke Snider, Gil Hodges, Pee Wee Reese, Roy Campanella, Carl Furillo, and Jackie Robinson. These were the Dodgers of Flatbush.

As the Los Angeles Dodgers entered the 1960s, gone were most of the Boys of Summer. Left were only a couple of aging past their prime—stars like Hodges and Snyder. Gone was cozy Ebbets Field, replaced by the Los Angeles Coliseum, which held over ninety thousand fans the previous year for a single game. Once again in 1962, transition would move the team to yet another home field, Dodger Stadium. Celebrities, movie and television stars, sunshine, and the palm trees of Los Angles replaced the comfortable Brooklyn working-class neighborhoods and the guy next door. The difference was as pronounced as the difference between the old Eisenhower presidency and the newly elected JFK administration.

These new Dodgers gave everyone a preview in 1959 of what was to be the their new future and how they would play baseball. That year they won the pennant after finishing in a first-place tie with Milwaukee, earning an NL playoff victory against a superior (on paper) Braves team featuring Hall of Famers like Hank Aaron, Eddie Mathews, and Warren Spahn. These new Dodgers scraped for runs and pitched their way not only past the Braves, but to a world championship by defeating the Go-Go Sox from Chicago. It would be this type of baseball in Los Angeles that would be so different from those big bats of Brooklyn. It would be the Dodger pitchers of the 1960s that would become the household names, not the hitters. Yes, things were different on and off the field from the 1950s and from Brooklyn, but the championships continued.

WHERE'S THE BEEF?

Beef-O-Meter, 1960–1964

In the sixties in Los Angeles, there was no beef. Most beloved baseball buffs outside of LA would be hard pressed to name more than a couple of people who hit 3-4-5 for the Dodgers during any given year at any time through the entire decade.

In 1960, Wally Moon hit in the third spot 76 times. Norm larker hit 61 times in the fourth hole, and Willie Davis hit fifth 39 times. As a side note, Junior Gilliam led off 94 times, as opposed to Maury Wills, who led off only 60 times that year, and Duke Snider hit fourth only 35 times !

The most consistent years for the Dodgers, which tends to be a barometer for most teams when it comes to winning results, was in the early part of the decade, in 1962, when Willie Davis hit third 118 times, Tommy Davis hit fourth 126 times, and Ron Fairly hit 70 times in the fifth spot. Another possible choice could have been in 1963, when Wally Moon hit third 56 times, Davis hit 112 times at cleanup, and Fairly was fifth in the lineup 60 times. It was during this time that slugging Frank Howard was being added more and more to the middle of the lineup. However, Tommy Davis suffered a severe injury that would take away his greatness during the rest of his career, and the injury began to limit his playing time. This would reduce any added growth from the emerging Howard.

Score = W. Davis 1, T. Davis 2, F. Howard 2 = Total 5

Score = W. Davis 1, F. Howard 2, R. Fairly 1 = Total 4

> "The Dodgers are such a .500 team that if there was a
> way to split a three-game series, they'd find it!"
> —Vin Scully, Dodgers announcer

Beef-O-Meter, 1965–1969

The Dodgers' middle of the lineup was so poor by 1968 that Willie Davis hit third 41 times, Tom Haller was 54 times in the cleanup spot, and Ron Fairly hit fifth 51 times. Tom Haller was a lifetime .257 hitter and hit only 25 home runs in four years as a Dodger—in over 1,600 at bats!

During the average year in this period, the Dodgers rate a two or three on the Beef-O-Meter. Nonetheless, there were years later in the decade when the Dodgers had Tom Haller, Jim Lefebvre, and Andy Kosko as the cleanup guy.

Score = W. Davis 1, No main quality hitter 0, Fairly 1 = Total 2

ANALYSIS

The Dodgers of the 1960s were nothing like their predecessors of the 1950s, a team built on outstanding hitting and power. In fact, the Dodgers were so inconsistent offensively that during five different years in the decade, they had the same one thru eight hitters only seven times or less in any one of those years!

As a kid, I remember that the Dodger attack was Wills walking or bunting his way to first. Next he would steal second. Gilliam would then sacrifice him to third. Finally, one of the Davis boys would hit a run-scoring fly ball. This was usually followed by a Koufax or Drysdale shutout For a score of Dodgers 1, opponent 0. Now, if you were facing the Cardinals and Bob Gibson that night, who worked in a hurry, you could have dinner reservations at 10:00 PM for an 8:05 game—and you'd be early!

Despite always scoring fewer runs in a year than the other NL power teams, the Dodgers won three pennants and two World Series during the decade. With this amount of success, and so little beef in the middle of the lineup, it would be easy to conclude by taking a closer look that Maury Wills had even a bigger impact on the Dodgers success than many might think. Furthermore one must credit the amazing Dodger pitching staff. How many times did Sandy Koufax, Don Drysdale, Stan Williams, Johnny Podres, Larry Sherry, Don Sutton, and others pitch well and lose close games due to an anemic offense? What could Koufax's and Drysdale's win-loss records really have been like?

One must conclude that when it came to the beef, it wasn't in Los Angeles in the 1960s. It doesn't matter if we look at 1960–1964 or 1965–1969. It wasn't very good at best, and it only got worse later in the decade. When it came to winning, the Dodgers maximized their talent, winning three World Series and four pennants from 1959–1966. And don't forget they were winning that deciding third game of the 1962 playoff game against the Giants going into the ninth inning, before losing that pennant.

SANDY KOUFAX AND DON DRYSDALE

"The trick against Drysdale is to hit him before he hits you."
—Orlando Cepeda

"I can see how he won twenty-five games. What
I don't understand is how he lost five!"
—Yogi Berra, on Sandy Koufax

After being a longtime advocate of the greatness of Sandy Koufax, I found even a greater appreciation of his achievements in the 1960s. Furthermore, the career of Don Drysdale and the other Dodger hurlers of the decade seem to have taken on a much-elevated position for me after reviewing the support from the "no meat" of their lineup. Outside the likes of Willie Davis, often-injured Tommy Davis, and a couple of Frank Howard years, this staff had very little support. The team played small ball with a run here and a run there, so Dodger pitchers had very little wiggle room for mistakes. Just how many more games would they have won, if they had had a Willie Mays, Willie McCovey, and Orlando Cepeda middle of the order, like Juan Marichal and Gaylord Perry enjoyed in San Francisco? How good were the Johnny Podres, Stan Williams, Larry Sherry, Claude Osteens, Bill Singers, and Don Suttons? What would their career numbers look like with some offensive beef to help out on occasion?

Sandy Koufax lost 27 games over 4 seasons from 1963–1966. His ERA was 1.88, 1.74, 2.04, and 1.73 during that stretch, and he pitched 31 shutouts. His postseason career numbers were 57 innings pitched. He had 61 strikeouts, and two of his eight starts were shutouts. His World Series ERA was 0.95—but his record was 4–3!

Don Drysdale had a lifetime ERA of 2.95. He pitched 49 shutouts and completed 167 of his 465 lifetime starts. He had six 200-plus strikeout seasons. He set the record for consecutive scoreless innings in 1968. He had only two 20-win-game seasons, and only six of his fourteen seasons resulted in more than 15 wins!

TO COOPERSTOWN OR NOT ... THAT IS THE QUESTION!

The 1960s were a time when so many superstars and Hall of Famers started, ended, or continued their careers. It would be hard to find any other decade in baseball history that could match it. Consider the stars, from Ted Williams and Stan Musial to Willie, Mickey, and the Duke. Although there were so many greats that played, and it was such a wonderful time for the fans, it was a very tough time for some stars to get their deserved recognition. Players like Vada Pinson, Tony Oliva, Jim Kaat, Tommy John, Rocky Colavito, Ken Boyer, and Maury Wills were among this group. Playing in almost any other decade would have gotten them the Cooperstown nod. These were great ballplayers. The worst thing that they did was play their outstanding careers in the shadows of so many baseball icons. A perfect example of someone who was overshadowed was Don Drysdale of the Dodgers. Drysdale was one of the best ever in the game. Yet because he was on the same staff as Sandy Koufax, he certainly did not get the notoriety that Koufax enjoyed. Drysdale by no means was a third-tier Hall of Famer. It was his misfortune to not only play at a time that the Gibsons, Marichals, and Koufaxes ruled the mound, but he was also on the same staff with one of these legendary players. Many of the above players stood in the shadows of baseball legends that were so far ahead of everyone in the game, it made others' game seem less than what it truly was. Can you imagine being Vada Pinson? He had to live in the shadows of the great Frank Robinson, when they were with the Reds. He must have gotten used to it, since they were on the same high school team, too!

There clearly is a case to be made for allowing players in the Hall who are so-called class C or tier three candidates. If the position is taken that it is for only the elite in baseball history, then any tier-two Hall of

Famers like Brooks Robinson, Don Drysdale, Billy Williams, or Lou Brock should not be enshrined, either. They were not the Aarons, Ruths, or Cobbs of the game, but they were truly fantastic players. To not have them in Cooperstown makes no sense. By allowing a Ron Santo or a Bill Mazeroski—who by most accounts are considered in that tier-three category—what did the Hall lose? In fact, what a shame it would have been to not recognize or have future generations not remember these players' careers and what they did for the game.

MAURY WILLS: NOT IN THE HALL?

Without Maury Wills, the Dodgers don't win the pennant in 1959, 1963, 1965, and 1966. They are not world champs in 1959, 1963, and 1965. Without Wills, they don't play a three-game postseason playoff against the Giants in 1962.

Maury Wills was the Dodger offensive of the 1960s. After looking at their anemic beef, it becomes quite obvious just how important he was. Willis brought base stealing to the National League in the 1960s like Hall of Famer Luis Aparicio did in the American League in the '50s. Wills' 104 stolen bases in 1962 helped him outpace Willie Mays of the pennant-winning Giants for the league's MVP honors. Wills won two Gold Gloves in addition to his 1962 MVP award. He was a five-time All Star. In his career he stole 586 bases, hit .281, had 2,134 hits, and scored 1,067 runs. Maury Wills' championship contributions are certainly overlooked when compared to that of Hall of Famer Bill Mazeroski's. Regardless of his overall greatness, I'll bet Wills would have rather hit a walk-off HR in the bottom of the ninth in the 1960 World Series instead!

SAN FRANCISCO GIANTS

A S A KID, I MUST confess that I made money while stalking Willie Mays. This was not a felony at the time, and I was young, but it did go unnoticed, anyway. It was okay because I did it to Hank Aaron, Roberto Clemente, and a host of other sluggers in the National League at the time.

To clarify this, I worked as a peanut vendor at Saint Louis's Busch Memorial Stadium during the 1960s. My goal was always to make sure that I was pedaling my wares in the field box section just as my heroes appeared in the on-deck circle. I would continue my leisurely selling in the section near the backstop until the conclusion of their at bat. Miraculously as the inning ended and they went out to the field, the fans in the bleachers had worked up an appetite! This rotation system worked wonderfully well for years, and I made a couple bucks and had my idols at my beck and call!

The first of the two 1961 All Star games was played in San Francisco's Candlestick Park on July 11. It is not remembered for the National League's come-from-behind victory: in extra innings, Roberto Clemente drove in Willie Mays with the winning run, making Giant's pitcher Stu Miller the winner. However, that's not what Miller is most noted for on that day. As 44,115 fans watched in the top of the ninth inning, a gust of wind appeared to blow the 165-pound Miller off the mound in the middle of his windup. Regardless of whether or not this is exaggerated, it makes a good story, and it does describe Candlestick.

Like the Dodgers, the New York Giants left the Polo Grounds and New York for the West Coast in 1958. They too would find themselves in a ballpark (Candlestick) for the 1960s that would be difficult for hitters. Unlike the Dodgers, the Giants would follow their tradition of decent pitching and great hitting. Instead of the Monte Irvines and Bobby Thompsons of the fifties, it would be Willie McCovey, Orlando Cepeda, and others, coupled with the great Willie Mays, for the 1960s. Yet it would be the Giants who not only would be the biggest underachievers of the decade, but perhaps in baseball history!

The Giants finished third or better eight of ten times in the 1960s. They finished second five years in a row (1965–1969). They won more games than any other team in baseball in the National League during the decade. They scored 650 more runs than the Dodgers during the 1960s. They had three Hall of Famers in the middle of their batting order and two Hall of Fame starters on their pitching staff for most of the ten-year period. Had it not been for a ninth inning rally of the third and deciding playoff game against the Dodgers in 1962, they would have not even won a pennant. They did *not* win the World Series when they did make it, and they even lost it at home in Game 7!

WHERE'S THE BEEF?

Beef-O-Meter, 1960–1964

From 1960 thru 1964 the Giants batting order was Willie Mays 3rd, Orlando Cepeda and Willie McCovey with the latter interchanging between the 4th and 5th spots. All three would be future Hall of Famers. Filling in between rests and injuries would be Felipe Alou, another All Star player. On the bench the likes of Matty Alou, a future NL batting champ. At the top of lineup was former AL batting champ Harvey Kuenn. By 1964 Jim Ray Hart, another home run slugger would be in the mix batting in the 5 hole 58 games that year and freeing Felipe Alou to the leadoff spot.

Score = Mays 3, McCovey 3, Cepeda 3, quality replacement Alou 1 = Total 10

> "I think I was the best player I ever saw."
> —Willie Mays

Beef-O-Meter, 1965–1969

From 1965 thru 1969 Mays continued batting 3rd most of the time, McCovey 4th and Hart 5th. An injured Orlando Cepeda was dealt to St Louis, only to rebound and win MVP honors in 1967. It was during this period the Giants finished in 2nd place every year.

Score= Mays 3, McCovey 3, Hart 2= Total Score 8

ANALYSIS

As a young boy, there was nothing like the San Francisco Giants and Willie Mays coming to town. He was surrounded by McCovey, Cepeda, Jim Ray Hart, and others, so you knew that you were in for some power thrills. In retrospect, what you were really seeing was one of the greatest disappointments in baseball history. Some things are hard to explain. Here was a team with Willie Mays, Orlando Cepeda, Willie McCovey, Juan Marichal, and Gaylord Perry—all future Hall of Famers, all in their prime. Second-line All Star players included Felipe Alou, Matty Alou, Jim Davenport, Tom Haller, Harvey Kuenn, Jim Ray Hart, Mike McCormick, Jack Sanford, Stu Miller, and Billy O'Dell. The 1960s organization rookies included Bobby Bonds, George Foster, Manny Mota, Jose Cardenal, and Randy Hundley. Most of the time the Giants featured three Hall of Famers in the middle of the lineup, and with only a four-man pitching rotation, they had a Hall of Fame pitcher on the mound every other night in either Marichal or Perry. Certainly the winds of Candlestick not only favored the home team Giants but often intimidated visiting ball clubs. Giants, I have to ask you: How in the hell did you not win?

Like I said, some things are beyond explanation. The Pet Rock, Silly Putty, Woodstock, and the 1960s Giants. Enough said!

GIANTS VERSUS DODGERS

An investigative look at the difference between the Dodgers and the Giants sheds some light as to why the Dodgers were able to produce so many championships and the Giants so little. Without a doubt the Giants had much more offense than the Dodgers. From 1960 to 1966, the Dodgers won three pennants and two world championships; the Giants won only the one. During this period the Giants outscored the Dodgers every year. In 1961 and 1962, the Giants gave up fewer runs than the Dodger pitchers did. On defense, their team fielding numbers were about equal, as the Dodgers led three of the years, and the Giants led three other years, with both teams finishing in a tie in 1963 at a .975 team fielding clip. The Dodgers normally had more double plays than the Giants in a season, but they were not usually among the NL leaders. All in all, with the Giants having to play half of their games in the swirling winds of Candlestick Park—which would diminish their fielding stats—they probably were the better fielding team of the two. So what is the difference?

Looking at the number of low-scoring games won, where the opposition scored two runs or less, reveals that in every year except 1960, the Dodgers had the edge. In 1960, the Giants had 57 games to the Dodgers' 56 in this category. But in 1962, it was the Dodgers by a 61–44 margin, and in 1963 it was LA by a whopping 76–44 difference over the Giants. That year the Dodgers had 24 shutouts to San Francisco's 9. They had 29 other games where they allowed only one run; the Giants had only 17. That meant that LA had 53 games to the Giants' mere 26 of one-run games or less. The trend continued, and by 1966 the Dodgers had 80 games—nearly half the season—where they gave up two runs or less; this included 20 shutouts.

On paper, the Giants offered more power and scored more runs. Defensively, they were better than the Dodgers because their fielding percentages were equal with the Dodgers, even though their home ballpark reduced their numbers. Their pitching was good because they had 81 shutouts to the Dodgers' 117 from 1960–1966. But in the final analysis, the Dodgers won the small ball, low-scoring games more often. It is as if they had an attitude that every run was hard to come by, and there might not be another one. The Giants knew that with their lineup, the next run was only one swing away. It seems that the Dodgers were more intense on every pitch. When they fell four to five runs behind, it was over. The Giants knew that the next inning, they could make a four-run differential disappear. The Dodgers got it done and won the games when they needed to; they rose to the occasion when it counted. The Giants didn't do that and became the decade's also-ran.

SAINT LOUIS CARDINALS

"A couple of years ago they told me I was too young to be president
and you were too old to be playing baseball ... But we fooled them!"
—John F. Kennedy to Stan Musial, at the 1962 All Star Game

IN 1960s SAINT LOUIS, AS a kid it was impossible to go without
listening to Harry Caray every night. (Yes, believe it or not, he spent
many more years as a Saint Louis announcer than he did as a Cubs
announcer.) Overzealous and enthusiastic in style, he made his longtime
partner, Hall of Fame announcer Jack Buck, seem rather reserved.
Caray pronounced Stan the Man's last name as "Moosuual," and he was
constantly full of entertaining baseball antics—things like having a net
in the broadcast booth in which to catch foul balls. His description of
"There's a drive way back, it might be out of here, it could be ... It is! A
home run! Holy Cow!" is something that all fans of the time will take
to their graves. As exciting as he always made it seem, when I took my
transistor to the game, his embellishment of what I was actually seeing
on the field was a disconnect. Regardless, at 8:05 every night it was
Cardinal baseball and not ice cream that I wanted!

While growing up in Saint Louis in the sixties, I had the opportunity to
witness some lifelong memories that I treasure to this date. Starting in
1963, the great Stan the Man Musial retired. A godlike icon to the Saint

Louis community, his final at bat and his final hit (a ground ball in the hole between first and second beyond a diving rookie named Pete Rose, who would later pass Musial's all time number of hits), and his final jog to the dugout that day will always be embedded in my mind. The next year, 1964 was the great Phillies collapse, and the Cardinals beat the Yankees in Game 7 with a worn-out Bob Gibson putting the nails in the coffin of New York's forty-year dynasty. The year 1965 introduced us with the Gateway to West, as the Saint Louis Arch was completed. I had mixed emotions in May of 1966 as the legendary Sportsman's Park closed for the new Busch Memorial Stadium. I went to the last game with 17,502 fans at Sportsman's Park that Sunday on May 8, against the San Francisco Giants. A power show featuring home runs from Willie McCovey, Jim Ray Hart, and of course the very last home run hit there by any player in Willie Mays in the ninth to right field resulted in a score of Giants 10, Cardinals 5.

Then I went to the second game at the new Busch Stadium against the Atlanta Braves. The Birds won there! In only a couple of years, I was honored and went to work as a vendor at the new stadium. This gave me the chance to see hundreds of games and all my heroes up close. In 1967, El Birdos were back by beating the Red Sox in Game 7; once again, a tiring Bob Gibson closed out the series victoriously for the Cards that year. Saint Louis was back again to the World Series in 1968, this time against the Detroit Tigers. Gibson again won Game 1 with strikeout heroics. Although we didn't win that series, we did win three pennants and two world championships in those years. That was the Cardinals and Saint Louis through the eyes of a kid in the 1960s.

WHERE'S THE BEEF?

Beef-O-Meter, 1960–1964

The Cardinal beef during the first half of the decade was Bill White hitting third, Ken Boyer fourth, and sometimes Stan Musial hitting fifth or being interchanged in the third or fourth spot. When Musial retired in 1963, Dick Groat moved in and out of the third and fifth spot. In 1963, the Cardinals used the exact starting eight in the lineup nine times during the season; they finished second to the Los Angeles Dodgers. The following year, they used the same exact starting lineup some nineteen times, proving consistency in the order is an element to success, because they won the World Series.

White was an excellent ballplayer and a good RBI slugger, so he was two points. Ken Boyer was greatly underrated and was possibly a tier-three Hall of Famer, so he's worth two points. Although Musial was one of baseball's greats, he was in the twilight of his career and was only worth one point. Dick Groat, former MVP and batting champion, was one point.

Score = Boyer 2 plus, White 2, Groat/Musial 1 plus = Total 5 or 6

"Bob Gibson is the luckiest pitcher I ever saw. He always pitches when the other team doesn't score any runs."

—Tim McCarver

Beef-O-Meter, 1965–1969

In the second half of the 1960s, the Cardinal lineup looked completely different from the White-Boyer-Musial/Groat order that the Birds rode the first half of the decade. The presence of Curt Flood, Hall of Famer Orlando Cepeda, clutch-hitting Roger Maris, and Tim McCarver was the bulk of the years for the middle of the lineup in 1966 through 68. Curt Flood moved to second in the order, following Lou Brock, after hitting third in 1965 and 1966. The decade ended with a Vada Pinson/Joe Torre/Tim McCarver look.

Cepeda was a Hall of Famer and was three points. Flood was a consistent .290–.300 hitter and was two points. McCarver was one point. Maris had lost his power and was near the end of his career, so he was one point.

Score = Flood 2, Cepeda 3, McCarver 1 = Total 6

Score = Maris 1, Cepeda 3, McCarver 1 = Total 5

ANALYSIS

The Cardinals won three pennants and two World Series in the 1960s. Set lineups—like nineteen games in 1964, thirty-three games in 1967, and thirty-four games in 1968—seemed to be the key. Four times the team finished fifth or worse in the standings in other years. Balance seemed to be the key with the Cardinals, with adequate hitting, good pitching, solid defense, and speed; a ball park that was conducive to those benefits didn't hurt, either.

Player analyses are as follows. Ken Boyer was MVP in the National League in 1964. He is often overlooked as to how good he was. Next was the great Bob Gibson. How many more games would Gibson have won with a better hitting club? How many more would he have had in 1968, when he led the league with a 1.12 ERA yet lost an incredible nine games? When the game was on the line, you wanted Gibson on the mound. Orlando Cepeda ignited the Cardinals with his presence and won an MVP in '67.

However, if there exists a common denominator with the team from the 1964 championship through the 1968 NL champs, it would be that the middle of the lineup was good but not great. By 1964 the Cardinals had had the same middle lineup for several of the prior seasons, yet they had not won; that rated a five on our Beef-o-Meter. In 1967 and 1968, the players were different in the middle but were still a five or six. What became evident in both cases was that the juice came from the top of the lineup. The ability of Lou Brock to get on and get into scoring position made the difference, both as a newcomer in mid-1964 and again in 1967–1968 .His impact on the Cardinals was very much like that of Maury Wills for the Dodgers: get on and get in. In fact the two teams were similar in many ways. The biggest differences were that the Dodgers had slightly better pitching, and the Birds had slightly better hitting. Both scratched for runs, and both won three pennants and won two world championships. These two teams dominated the National League during the decade. In the final analysis, for a team with consistent batting lineups and consistent, quality pitching and solid defense, the Cards were everything *but* consistent—they finished all over the board in the final standings through the 1960s

LOS ANGELES DODGERS VERSUS SAINT LOUIS CARDINALS

As successful as the Dodger and Cardinal teams were, they rated average to below average in comparison to some of the other power NL beef in the middle of the their orders. In retrospect, it was the top of the order in both cases that made the difference. Without Brock coming to the Cardinals from the Cubs in a midseason 1964 trade, in all likelihood they would not have won in any of the years. However, Flood should not be overlooked because he covered for Brock's defensive mediocrity in left field, and he moved him like a puzzle piece around the diamond for Redbird tallies offensively.

Similarly, the Dodgers, who ranked low in the middle of the, manufactured runs like the Cardinals with Maury Wills and Jim Gilliam. Wills bunted for a hit or walked, and then by stealing second he was easily pushed to third by the switch-hitting Gilliam. A fly ball, ground out, wild pitch, or sometimes even a hit would give the Dodgers a lead, and the pitching would make it hold up for the win. It would be safe to say that without Wills, the Dodgers may have never made it to the World Series. His role was so important to their success that it's hard to imagine he isn't in Cooperstown like his friendly foe Lou Brock

KEN BOYER: NOT IN THE HALL?

In Saint Louis the only player pictured on the outfield walls at Busch Stadium not in Cooperstown is Ken Boyer. Boyer's career preceded Ron Santo's for a short time, and Boyer was Santo's contemporary rival in the early 1960s. During his career, Boyer won five Gold Gloves at third base, and eight times he hit over 20 home runs. In 1964 he was the NL MVP, and it was Boyer's grand slam in Game 4 of the 1964 World Series that turned the tide for a Redbird championship over the New York Yankees. Boyer hit .287 with 1,141 RBI and 282 home runs during his career. He had a nearly forty-year–old, declining Stan Musial and a decent hitter in Bill White for his protection. He did not have the advantage of Santo in Billy Williams and Ernie Banks. He did not play half of his

games in a windy Wrigley Field. Although the two had similar careers, only Santo is in the Hall of Fame. Ken Boyer died in his early fifties and did not get the opportunity to remind people of his greatness by just being around. The people in Saint Louis know something the rest of the baseball world should know.

CURT FLOOD: NOT IN THE HALL?

Like Reds star Vada Pinson, Curt Flood played at a time when the legends of the game roamed the NL outfields. Unlike Pinson, Flood won seven Gold Gloves. That was amazing, considering that each year, two of three outfield awards were probably taken in advance by Clemente and Mays. However, many considered Flood to be the best defensive outfielder in the game. In 1966 he went the whole season without an error. His streak of 226 errorless games became a record, along with 568 consecutive errorless chances. Two times the three-time All Star had over 200 hits in a season, leading the league in 1964. Flood helped lead the Cardinals to the 1964 and 1967 world championships. He also helped them to the 1968 pennant. His career numbers of 1,861 hits would have been substantially higher had he not refused to be traded to the Phillies at the end of the decade and quit baseball. His stance on free agency— that players were not property, like slaves—was not accepted by baseball owners. Flood was committed to his beliefs and stood his ground, taking his case all the way to the United States Supreme Court. In the meantime, he lost his $100,000 a year salary, went bankrupt, and all but ended his career. He never achieved lifetime Hall of Fame numbers as a result. His impact on the game and on players lives on today. Whether or not you like his actions, Curt

Flood had a fingerprint both on and off the field. Isn't that what the Hall of Fame is about?

"I am a human being. I am not a piece of property.
I am not a consignment of goods."
—Curt Flood

"I was told by the general manager that a white player
had received a higher raise than me: because white people
required more money to live than black people."
—Curt Flood

"I am glad God made my skin black. I just
wish he had made it a little thicker.
—Curt Flood

"I lost money, coaching jobs and a shot at the Hall of Fame."
—Curt Flood

CINCINNATI REDS

IN OAKLAND, AT McCLYMONDS HIGH School in the mid-1950s, the Cincinnati Reds signed three of the school's outfielders. One would go on to Cooperstown, and the other two should have. Between them they would combine for 7,561 major league hits and over 3,500 RBIs, plus 927 home runs! The kids were Frank Robinson (who also played on the basketball team with the legendary Bill Russell), Vada Pinson, and Curt Flood.

The Cincinnati Reds entered the 1960s as one baseball's worst teams since World War Two; only once since then had they finished as high as third place. Most of the time they dwelled in the bottom half of the National League, and they were not very competitive. In the fifties, they were even forced to change their logo to the Red Legs for a few years, in response to the connotations and association of the name Reds to that of communism and Senator Joe McCarthy's witch hunt.

The Reds finished the 1960 season in sixth place with a record of 67–87. In 1961, they went to the World Series. The turnaround came as a result of a strong pitching staff, with Jim O'Toole, Joe Jay, and Bob Purkey. Equally important was the maturing of slugging combo Vada Pinson (who would move from second to third in the order) and future Hall of Famer Frank Robinson. They would finish third in 1962, although they won 98 games. They had a second-place finish in 1964, only a game behind the Cardinals, due to losing the final game of the season. They would finish fourth three other times and seventh once, before a third place finish in 1969.

After the 1965 season, the Reds traded what they called an "old" thirty-year-old Frank Robinson to Baltimore, for, essentially Milt Pappas. (Even when I was eleven years old, this didn't make sense to me. Did this mean that I only had nineteen more years left of quality life in front of me, before old age set in?) Robinson went on to win the Triple Crown and the AL MVP in 1966 for the Orioles. The Reds scored 133 runs less in 1966 compared to the previous year.

The 1960s were one of player development for the team. The Reds brought up Pete Rose, Tony Perez, Johnny Bench, Tommy Harper, Jim Maloney, Lee May, and Tommy Helms. May and Helms would be traded to get Hall of Famer Joe Morgan. It was this group of rookies that would set the table for the Big Red Machine of the 1970s. Despite the wealth of new talent the Reds had, it would be the Frank Robinson trade that broke their back during the second half of the decade and postpone their upcoming success.

WHERE'S THE BEEF?

Beef-O-Meter, 1960–1964

Score = Vada Pinson 2, Frank Robinson 3, Gordy Coleman/Deron Johnson 1 = Total 6

Robinson was an elite Hall of Fame slugger. Pinson was an outstanding player who should be a tier-three Hall of Famer. Gordy Coleman and Deron Johnson were productive with some power and were solid at one point.

> "How can anyone as slow as you pull a muscle?"
> —Pete Rose, to Tony Perez

Beef-O-Meter, 1965–1969

Score = Pinson 2, Robinson/Perez 3, D. Johnson/L. May 1 = Total 6

Pinson was excellent. Robinson and Perez were Hall of Famers. Johnson and May were both good sluggers.

ANALYSIS

The Reds of the 1960s had an outstanding hitting team. With the meat being Pinson, Robinson, Perez, Bench, May, and Johnson, combined with Pete Rose at the top of the order, the team scored over 800 runs in two seasons and 798 in another. They started the decade with excellent pitching; by the middle to the end of the 1960s, the Reds pitching was average, and the team would mostly be known for its great hitting for many years to come.

In retrospect, the Robinson trade looms big. So lost were the Reds after the trade that the number four hitter in the order for 1966 was filled the most by Gordy Coleman, in only 53 games. The five hole was held by Art Shamsky and Deron Johnson, both hitting there 37 times each. The Reds became so desperate while waiting for their young talent to mature that they moved a diminishing Vada Pinson to the second spot and dropped Pete Rose to the third spot.

VADA PINSON: NOT IN THE HALL?

Pinson had 2,757 hits with 256 home runs, 1,170 RBI, and 305 stolen bases to go with his .286 lifetime batting average. He had seven 20-plus home run seasons. He scored 100 runs in four different seasons. He had 200-plus hits in a season four times. He won a Gold Glove in 1961 and helped lead the Reds to a pennant. He led the National League two times in hits, two times in doubles, two times in triples, and two times in at bats. He was an All Star only twice; this was an indication of being in the wrong place at the wrong time, and being overshadowed by playing at the same time as many of the immortals of the game.

Vada Pinson is not in the Hall because of his own ability. He is not there because the Veteran's Committee overlooks his skills and makes comparisons to his contemporaries, like Hank Aaron, Willie Mays, Frank Robinson, and Roberto Clemente, who all were legendary icons. Vada Pinson is not a tier-three Hall of Famer—because he is probably a tier-two candidate! Wake up, world!

Chicago Cubs

"I'm an escaped car thief. I broke out of prison
to see the Cubs in the World Series."
—Jim Belushi, *Taking Care of Business*

W AVELAND AVENUE, WHICH SETS BEHIND the left field bleachers in Chicago's famous Wrigley Field, could have easily gotten its name from the Cubs hurlers waving good-bye to their fastballs as they left the park throughout the decade.

Going into the 1960s, the Chicago Cubs had had a history of being bad. From 1939 to 1969, the team had finished above third only one time. In fact, only once from 1939 to 1967 did they even finish third. The Cubs had not been world champions since before the *Titanic* sank! So what about the sixties? In 1961, the Cubs had 5 future Hall of Famers in the lineup. The next year they would have four future Hall of Famers plus the rookie of the year—and they finished 59–103! They finished ninth that year, behind Houston, even though the Colt 45s were an expansion team! For most of the decade, they would have at least four future Hall of Famers plus sometimes a Hall of Fame manager in Leo Durocher. They opened the decade finishing seventh, seventh, ninth, seventh, eighth, eighth, eighth, and tenth. Despite the Hall of Famers and all the rookies of the year, the Cubs pitching was hit so hard that it was hard to tell if the game was being played, or the opposition was just taking batting practice. Often they were one in the same.

WHERE'S THE BEEF?

Beef-O-Meter, 1960–1964

During the 1960s, the Cubs boasted three future Hall of Famers in the middle of their lineup: Billy Williams, Ron Santo, and Ernie Banks. George Altman, a capable regular, would be in the middle when the others were rested.

Score = Williams 3, Santo 3, Banks 3, Altman as a quality replacement 1 = Total 10

> "The Cubs are due in sixty-two."
> —Ernie Banks

> "The Cubs are gonna shine in sixty-nine."
> —Ernie Banks

> "The only way to prove that you're a good sport is to lose."
> —Ernie Banks

> "It's a great day for a ball game; let's play two!"
> —Ernie Banks

Beef-O-Meter, 1965–1969

Again it was Williams, Santo, and Banks every year during this time, without any measurable replacements.

Score = Williams 3, Santo 3, Banks 3 = Total 9

ANALYSIS

Chicago Cubs fans had to be a dedicated bunch in the sixties. The Cubs were outscored by their opposition every year from 1960 to 1966; three times they gave up over 800 runs in a year. In 1962, they gave up 827 runs while scoring 632—that's almost 200 runs less! They had two years where they lost more than 100 games in a year—and this was after the Mets and Houston were added to the league! In 1961 they had five Hall of Famers on the roster: Billy Williams, Ernie Banks, Ron Santo, Lou Brock, and Richie Ashburn. The following year Ashburn was gone, but they added Ken Hubbs, who became rookie of the year. During those two years, they won 123 and lost 193.

In 1964, disaster hit the Cubs as promising future star Ken Hubbs would die in a plane crash in February. In the summer, they would trade future Hall of Famer Lou Brock to the Cardinals in one of baseball history's most lopsided trades.

As the Cubs improved their pitching staff with stars like Fergie Jenkins, Bill Hands, and Ken Holtzman, they began to rise in the standings. This once again shows the importance of pitching, as the middle of the Cub lineup remained the same. In 1966 they finished tenth, but in 1967 and 1968 they finished third both times. All Cubs fans like to say that in 1969, they had a big lead late in the year but lost it to the future world champion Mets, finishing a close second. The reality is they finished eight games behind the Mets that year.

The Cubs are a great example of how a team with three Hall of Famers consistently in the middle of the lineup (Williams, Santo, and Banks hit in the same spot almost every game from 1963–1969) with little to no pitching can constantly be a bottom dweller. Yes, they did have the beef; those three combined would hit nearly 1,300 home runs in their careers.

When looking closer at the Cubs, it is amazing how many years and how many times Billy Williams would hit in the third spot in the order. From 1964 through 1969, Williams hit in that spot no less than 159 games every year. Likewise, Santo had a large number of games that he hit fourth, behind Williams and before Banks.

This brings up three questions. One, why was Williams always hitting third and not sometimes fifth, rather than the right-handed-hitting Banks, because the Cubs would face a number of opposing left-handed starters? Why did the team continue to stay with the same lineup?

The next question is, how good was Billy Williams, to be in that order year in and year out that many times? It is amazing as to how consistent and durable he was.

The last question is this: does Ron Santo really belong in the Hall of Fame? Sure, he was a good hitter and a multi–Gold Glove winner. However, of his 342 home runs (337 in the National League), a disproportional amount (212) were hit at the friendly confines of windy Wrigley Field, with only 125 on the road.

SAN FRANCISCO GIANTS AND CHICAGO CUBS

The two most underperforming teams in the National League during the 1960s were the San Francisco Giants and the Chicago Cubs. The Giants won more games than any other NL team during the decade. The middle of the lineup supported three future Hall of Famers in Willie Mays, Willie McCovey, and Orlando Cepeda—all of which were in the prime of their careers. In addition, they had the three Alous, Felipe, Matty, and Jesus. Others cast members included Harvey Kuene, Manny Mota, Jim Davenport, Tom Haller, Bobby Bonds, and "Sugar Bear" Jim Ray Hart. Then, we must also throw in two future Hall of Fame pitchers in Juan Marichal and Gaylord Perry, plus Stu Miller, strikeout ace Mike McCormick, and Billy Pierce. When you consider that half of their games each season were played in Candlestick Park, a definite advantage for the Giants, how did this team *not* win championships?

Similarly, the Chicago Cubs had a home field advantage by playing half of each season in Wrigley Field. They had three Hall of Famers in Billy Williams, Ron Santo, and Ernie Banks in the middle of their lineup; all three were in their prime for most of the decade. In addition, they had a future Hall of Famer in Fergie Jenkins on the mound every fourth day. The supporting cast included Hall of Famers Richie Asburn, Lou

Brock, and manager Leo Durocher. Oh, and don't forget 1962 rookie of the year second baseman Ken Hubbs.

Although the Cubs did not have as much talent as the Giants during the sixties, they finished seventh three times, eighth two times, ninth once, and even tenth once. Oh, did I mention that Sandy Koufax's perfect game came against the Cubs? Shame on you, Cubbies! Chicago deserved better!

CHICAGO CUBS: COLLEGE OF COACHES?

P. K. Wrigley was an icon in the chewing gum world. Two major league ball parks carried the family name in the early 1960s, one in Chicago (home to the Cubbies, which he owned), and one in Los Angeles, which was home to the newly formed American League Angels during their inaugural season, also called Wrigley Field. With that much infiltration in the majors, one would think that he was a genius to the baseball world. Nothing could have been further from the truth. His announcement prior to the 1961 season of his well-thought-out plan of the College of Coaches stands as living testimony to his incredible baseball ineptitude.

The College of Coaches was to be a rotation system of Chicago Cubs coaches, whereby each would take turns managing the Cubs as head coach. There was to be no manager, and each coach would take his turn without a definite time frame outlined. The front office would determine when the next head coach would be put in charge and for what length of tenure he would have. As a coach was replaced, he would either continue to be a Cubby coach, or he'd temporarily work in the minors until his turn in the rotation with the big league club came up again. This concept was given to Wrigley by Cubs backup catcher El Tappe, who happened to be one of the coaches in 1961 and again in 1962.

The results were disastrous. The Cubs were 64–90 in the 1961 season. Lou Klein's head coaching record was 5–6, Harry Craft was 7–9, Verdie Himsl was 10–21, and El Tappe was 42–54. As the coaches worked against each other, the Cubs on the field resented the program.

Not to be discouraged by 1961's results, and to avoid a rush to judgment, the Cubs attempted to try it again in 1962. That year they came back with Klein, Tappe, and Charlie Metro as head coaches. Klein was 12–18, Tappe was 4–16, And Metro was 43–69. The group managed the Cubs a 59–103 record! To add insult to injury, they finished six games behind the newly formed expansion Houston Colt 45s. By the end of the 1962 season, the experiment was scrapped, and the College of Coaches belonged to the ages.

Probably the biggest thing overlooked in the whole debacle was that one of the coaches during this time was the late Buck O'Neil. O'Neil was a star in the Negro Leagues who would later serve as one of the great ambassadors of the game until his death in 2007. He had actually become the first black coach in Major League Baseball. Although he had no on-field duties and was not part of the College of Coaches, his historic elevation to a coach in the majors went amazingly unnoticed. Despite always being overlooked for the Hall of Fame as well, O'Neil never faltered in his enthusiasm and love for the game. It was his leadership and campaign that allowed so many forgotten stars of the Negro Leagues to gain entrance to Cooperstown. His only failure was that he didn't campaign for himself, and to this day he is not immortalized with a Hall of Fame enshrinement.

> "Baseball is like church. Many attend, few understand."
> —Leo Durocher, manager

RON SANTO: IN THE HALL?

Ron Santo was a great guy and was loved by Cubs fans everywhere … but does he belong in the Hall? Santo hit 342 home run, drove in 1,331 RBI, and had a lifetime .277 batting average with some 2,254 hits. Add to that five Gold Gloves and a longtime broadcasting career, and there is much merit for his enshrinement. The downside to Santo is that he hit many more of his 342 home runs in Wrigley Field as opposed to on the road. He hit between two great Hall of Fame sluggers for the entire decade, as Billy Williams got on in front of him, and Ernie Banks hit behind him. With that protection he got to see a lot of fat pitches that he would otherwise have not seen. Nonetheless, considering he had diabetes throughout career, his performance on the field was remarkable. His efforts in raising millions of dollars for the disease was a testimony for his work off the field. Regardless, Santo does provide a reason that there is room for the third-tier players in the Hall of Fame. What a shame it would have been if future generations were left without the memories he gave us.

PITTSBURGH PIRATES

I GUESS WHEN YOU ARE A kid, you always want to envision yourself not only playing in the majors, but hitting the winning homer in the seventh game of a World Series. Of course it is with two out, the bases loaded, a 3–2 count, and your favorite team down by three runs. This is just part of the process of your love of the game. Included in the metamorphosis is that you learn to imitate your favorite players.

I was no different. If I was Willie Mays that day, I made sure my hat flew off as I went from first to third. If I was playing the outfield, I had to make a basket catch. On a different day I wore a Yankees helmet that I had put on top of my head with the palm of my hand. I limped to the plate with the knees of a ninety-year–old, not a nine-year-old. I even learned to switch hit. But when it came to Roberto, now, that was just a different deal. I would leap at outside pitches like a caged animal, to pound them into right field. I would run the bases and fling my arms to make sure that it ended with a fade-away or pop-up slide. If it was a home run, I pranced around the bases with my arms close to my body. I would always catch the routine fly ball below my waste. If the ball was hit in the corner, I would make sure that I delayed my arrival so that I could spin and throw. Oh, by the way, did I say my neck was always moving from side to side or rotating, no matter if I was hitting or on defense? I loved Roberto Clemente.

Anytime you have Roberto Clemente at his prime in the middle of your lineup for a decade, you are going to have an opportunity to win, or at least to be a better team. Entering the 1960s, the Pirates had not been to the World Series since 1927. But in 1960 that was about to change after finishing seventh and eighth every year from 1950–1957. With two maturing future Hall of Famers in Roberto Clemente and Bill Mazeroski, the Bucs would finish second in 1958 and fourth in 1959. In 1960 they would shock the National League with a "never give up" attitude and capture the pennant. In dramatic fashion, they would continue to rock the baseball world as the Pirates beat a heavily favored Yankees team in the seventh game of the 1960 World Series on Bill Mazeroski's legendary walk-off home run.

Unfortunately, Pittsburgh would have only the 1960 World Series to celebrate during the decade. The Pirates would finish no better than third and would finish sixth or worse five times the remainder of the time. Although the lineup would usually include three future Hall of Famers—in the form of Clemente, Mazeroski, and Willie Stargell—plus other stars like Matty Alou, Donn Clendenon, Dick Stuart, Bob Skinner, and Billy Virdon, the quality pitching that Pittsburgh enjoyed in the late 1950s and early 1960s was not there for most of the decade.

WHERE'S THE BEEF?

Beef-O-Meter, 1960–1964

Clemente hit third or fifth during this period. Bob Skinner hit in the three hole for 92 games in 1960 and for 116 games in 1962. Slugger Dick Stuart hit fourth from 1960–1962. Dick Groat (1960 batting champ and NL MVP) hit second during those years, including 161 games in 1962. In 1963, both Groat and Stuart were traded. So desperate were the Bucs for hitting that Mazeroski, who had been hitting eighth most of the previous three years, was moved to hit fourth more than anyone else for the '63 season. He responded by hitting 8 home runs, 52 RBI, a .245 average, and an OBP of .286 for the season. Stargell would fill that spot the next year and for most of the remainder of the sixties.

Score = Clemente 3, Stuart 2, Skinner 1 = Total 6

> "Roberto Clemente could field the ball in New
> York and throw out a guy in Pennsylvania."
> —Vin Scully, Dodger broadcaster

Beef-O-Meter, 1965–1969

The lineup was stable with Clemente, Stargell, and Clendenon from 1965–1968. Clendenon was traded after 1968 and was replaced with Al Oliver, an upcoming star for 1969.

Score = Clemente 3, Stargell 3 Clendenon 1 or 2 = Total 7 or 8

Score = Clemente 3, Stargell 3, Oliver 2 = Total 8

ANALYSIS

The Pittsburgh Pirates were an average team in the 1960s, big on hitting and weak on pitching. But for one year, in 1960, they were a team of destiny that would be remembered in baseball history for one famous game in October.

Despite being better than they had been in the forties and fifties, the Pirates of the sixties could have been a better club had it not been for two trades for the 1963 season. First, former MVP shortstop Dick Groat was sent to Saint Louis, while at the same time the Pirates sent slugger Dick Stuart to Boston .So disastrous were these moves offensively that in 1962 the Pirates had scored 706 runs, and in 1963 they scored 567 runs. A Clemente, Mazeroski, and Clendenon middle of the lineup was held in check by opposing pitchers for the 1963 season.

The last half of the decade was very stable with Clemente, Stargell, and Clendenon regularly in the meat of the order. Add to the lineup a Matty Alou batting champion, a traded Maury Wills, and a great platoon and pinch hitter like Manny Mota, and despite that, the Pirates could do no better than third place from 1965–1969. It would not be until the 1970s when Pirate pitching—with Jerry Reuss, Bob Moose, Kent Tekulve, John Candelaria, and others—would support the Pittsburgh big hitters and thrust the Bucs into two world championships.

BILL MAZEROSKI: IN THE HALL?

There is little to argue that Maz's glove got him into the Hall of Fame. In fact, most people agree he was the best defensive second baseman in his era; many would argue that he may have been the best there ever was. However, if Hal Smith's eighth inning homerun in Game 7 of the 1960 World Series would have held up, Mazeroski would have never hit again in the game. Or, if Mickey Mantle doesn't make a great baserunning maneuver to avoid a double play in the top of the ninth in the same game, the Pirates win, and neither the Pirates or Mazeroski come to bat in the ninth. Bill Mazeroski hit in the seventh and eighth hole for a predominantly second-division team in the sixties. Mazeroski's career numbers of a .260 average, 138 home runs, and 853 RBI are not Cooperstown offensive stats. As mentioned, though, his defense was incomparable. He won eight Gold Gloves and set countless double play and defensive records. Nonetheless, without that bat in the bottom of the ninth in Forbes Field, he never sees the Hall.

PHILADELPHIA PHILLIES

In July 1965, the Phillies were caught in the middle of a racial controversy on the field, similar to that which swept the nation off the field as a whole. Often criticized for racial overtones and considered by some as a bully, Philadelphia outfielder Frank Thomas was accused of instigating a fight and using a bat on the Phillies rising black star Richie Allen. Allen wasn't new to racial overtones, and he had an outspoken attitude, so he willingly participated in the fight. Who was really at fault did not matter. Thomas was immediately traded, and Philly teammates were threatened with heavy fines if they didn't keep quiet or if they discussed the matter. Although Thomas appeared as the loser, Philly fans taunted Allen in the upcoming years with racial slurs and threw things at him from the stands. Allen began wearing his batting helmet not only at the plate but in the field. Eventually it became too much, and Allen asked to be traded.

Philly fans suffered each year from the end of World War One into the early 1960s, with only a few exceptions. The team finished in last place twenty times between 1918 and 1961. In that same span, the Phillies finished above fourth only three times. A lonely trip to the World Series in 1950 by the Whiz Kids resulted in a four-game sweep by the New York Yankees. Going into 1960, Philadelphia was coming off two consecutive last-place finishes in 1958 and 1959. They would continue in last the next two years, until they were saved by NL expansion in 1962, and by a new manager for the sixties, Gene Mauch. It would be under Mauch that the team would gain respect for the remainder of decade. Mauch would take a mediocre Phillies club to within one game of a pennant in 1964, only to lose the pennant to the surging Cardinals on the last day of the season. It was Mauch that had turned the team into a competitive franchise with just average talent. The team that had been so bad for over sixty years, without a World Series championship, had begun an about-face that started under him in 1962 with an 81–80 record. That record resulted in a seventh-place finish, but it was a great improvement over the 47–107 record of 1961. After Mauch's departure, the Phillies would go to through the next four decades making many postseason appearances and winning several championships.

WHERE'S THE BEEF?

Beef-O-Meter, 1960–1964

During this period the Phillies' meat of the order was in transition. In 1960 the Phillies had Johnny Callison, Pancho Herrera, and Ken Walters most of the time in the 3-4-5 spots. Herrera only played three total years in the bigs; by 1961 his career was over. He did lead the NL in strikeouts one year. The other not-household name was Walters, who had 11 homeruns and 58 RBI, and hit .231 for his career. He also had 6 stolen bases but was caught 7 times getting those career stats. In 1961, Walters was replaced by Don Demeter; the latter would have a couple good years for the Phillies and added more power. Little wonder why the team lost 202 games those two years, when teams were still playing a 154-game schedule.

Tony Gonzalez (a.286 lifetime hitter) was added to the third spot in 1962. Callison was moved to second in the order the next two years until 1964, when he was move to third for most of the rest of the 1960s. It was in 1964 that Richie Allen came to the fourth spot, followed by Wes Covington and Tony Gonzalez (who would primarily hit in that spot for two more years). Under Gene Mauch, the Phillies had become more consistent, using the same starting lineup 12 times in 1962, 13 times in 1963, 11 games in 1964, and 14 games in 1965. This provided more stability, and the Phils played over .500 every year during that stretch.

Score = Callison 2, Herrera 1, Walters 0 = Total 3

Score = Callison 2, Allen 3, Gonzalez 1 = Total 6

> "I'll play first, third, left. I'll play anywhere—except Philadelphia."
> —Richie Allen

Beef-O-Meter, 1965–1969

The Phillies entered into an era of stability in the middle of their lineup from 1965–1969. Each year Johnny Callison would hit third and Richie Allen would hit fourth (except in 1969, when they reversed positions in the order). In 1965 Tony Gonzalez would hit fifth. In 1966 the Phillies acquired slugger Bill White from the Cardinals; that year White and Gonzalez shared the spot. In 1967 and 1968, White hit in the fifth spot the most.

Score = Callison 2, Allen 3, Bill White/Gonzalez/Deron Johnson 1 = Total 6

ANALYSIS

The Phillies started the 1960s losing nearly 100 games. They ended the sixties by nearly losing a 100 games. In between, however, they finished over .500 six times and nearly won the pennant once. Not blessed with Hall of Famers other than Jim Bunning through a trade in 1964, the Phillies had an average hitting club (except for the Callison-Allen duo) and average pitching. Nothing could reveal this more than during the 1964 run for pennant. With twelve games left in the season, the Phillies had a six and a half game lead. They lost ten in a row. Faced with a club of average talent, Mauch started pitchers Jim Bunning and Chris Short in thirteen of the last twenty games, in desperation. Despite what Phillies fans call "The Collapse," they finished second. For the most part they finished the decade stable. Regardless, the Phillies had now positioned themselves for the seventies. Mike Schmidt, Steve Carlton, Greg Luzinski, Larry Bowa, Gary Matthews, and Gary Maddox would propel the Phillies to be future champion contenders.

GENE MAUCH: HERO OR SCAPEGOAT?

Gene Mauch will forever be remembered as the manager of the 1964 "Phillie Phold." It was a year where the Phillies lost a huge lead in the last two weeks to finish one game behind a surging Saint Louis Cardinals team. Likewise, Mauch had two other near-misses in the 1980s, one as the manager of the Twins and another as the Angels skipper in 1986; both teams would put Mauch within one game of going to the World Series. His career is remembered for these failures.

When he retired as manager, Mauch ranked eighth on the all-time winning list of managers, with 1,902 victories to his credit. This is quite an accomplishment, considering that he took over a Phillies team that had a franchise history of being really bad. When Mauch was thrown into the job as Philadelphia's manager to begin the 1960 season, the team's number four hitter was Pancho Herrera who was surrounded by a group of no names. The results were a disaster.

In 1961, the Phillies would lose 23 games in a row. However, in 1962 the effects of Mauch would start to show, and they finished above .500 with a record of 81–80, despite being outscored for the season by over 50 runs. In 1963 the Phillies climbed to fourth place with a record of 87–75. In 1964, they finished second, one game behind the Cardinals, losing a big lead for which Mauch was to be blamed for the rest of his life. In reality, the '64 team wasn't that great anyway, and Mauch probably got them much closer than they should have been. They had Richie Allen and Johnny Callison in the middle, who were good, but there weren't many household names to add to the two. The pitching staff was young and without a great deal of experience, except for Jim Bunning, a future Hall of Famer. Cal McLish, Ray Culp, Art Mahaffey, and Chris Short were all decent pitchers; but they were in the beginning of their careers. Mauch is often criticized for pitching Short and Bunning so much, with little or no rest down the stretch. The two pitchers were overworked and could not hold up, and the Phillies faded from what looked like a certain pennant. Why would he have pitched these two so much during such a critical time?

The 1964 Philadelphia Phillies did not fold, as many would think. They were simply exposed over the 162-game season. Mauch was forced to go repeatedly with his aces because he didn't have the talent for an entire season. No one mentions the offense. Why were they not able to win by sheer hitting, as the team folded day after day? They, too, were average at best, as it turns out. To say that the Phillies folded and collapsed is an injustice to Mauch, because he probably got them a lot closer than they should have been.

Gene Mauch would take a 1961 team that won only 47 games and have the Phillies play above .500 baseball for six consecutive years. In 1969, Mauch became the manager of the new expansion Montreal Expos. It is amazing that with the managing success that he had with the Phillies, Twins, and the Angels, in addition to winning nearly 2,000 games, his career is still often criticized.

Is It Richie or Dick?

Richie Allen *did not* hit home runs. Richie Allen hit moons shots! He hit the ball so far in the air that some people believe he is the reason for global warming today. Willie Stargell, the famous Pirate slugger, said in the 1975 *Baseball Digest* on page 36, "Now I know why they boo Richie all the time. When he hits a home run there is no souvenir."

Richie Allen was as controversial as Obama Care, and he was as outspoken as Rush Limbaugh. He seemed bound by his actions to be criticized by the media. He had been the target of racism in the minors while playing at Little Rock, Arkansas, the Phillies minor league affiliate. There fans called him racist names and jeered from the stands. Even though he had not been used to that, growing up near Pittsburgh, it still seemed to follow him to the majors. He was as talented at the plate as Mickey Mantle but more remembered for his controversy than his abilities.

Richie Allen won rookie of the year honors in 1964 when he hit .318 with 201 hits, 29 home runs, and 125 runs. When the Phillies were collapsing during the pennant drive, Allen hit .438 with 3 home runs and 11 RBI the last twelve games of the season. He won AL MVP honors in 1972. During his career he hit 351 home runs (some 20 completely out of Philadelphia's Connie Mack Stadium) and had 1,119 RBI.

Recently, in an interview with Bob Costas, Allen took responsibility for some of his attitude and actions. He was relaxed and sincere, and he came across as a very sweet individual. Where was Richie? This was Dick Allen, as he had been going by the last forty years or so. From all accounts, teammates and managers constantly remember him as a leader in the clubhouse, a great teammate, and someone who always busted their butt on the field. This was a completely different analysis from what the media had portrayed. Regardless of what they thought about Allen off the field, no one argued about his on-field ability.

Richie Allen strolled to the plate with a forty-plus ounce bat that was at least thirty-five inches. With that Allen swagger, he flipped his bat like a tooth pick in the box as he took opposing pitchers to a different time zone. As a kid, I loved to imitate him, though I could only do it with a Wiffle Ball bat. No one in the majors could use a wooden bat the way he did. He was simply amazing.

If introduced to him today, what would I call him, Richie or Dick? I think Mr. Allen would be more appropriate. Everyone that watched him play has his own Allen stories. Some are good and some are bad. I'm just glad he was part of my life.

> "If a horse won't eat it, I don't want to play on it."
> —Dick Allen, on Astro Turf

MILWAUKEE/ATLANTA BRAVES

E NTERING THE 1960S, THE MILWAUKEE Braves had by far been
the best NL team over the previous five years. They finished
second in 1955 and 1956, first in 1957 (world champs), first in 1958,
and second in 1959 (tied for first, lost playoff). The Braves were on a
roll entering the 1960s. In 1960 they finished second; in 1969 they
won the NL West. However, between 1961 and 1968, they were
bad. They finished fourth, fifth five times, sixth, and seventh during
that stretch. How could a team that had Hank Aaron in his prime,
and Eddie Mathews slightly past his, be so bad? This duo had 1,267
career home runs between them in their careers! Add Joe Adcock
and Joe Torre in the five hole behind these two Hall of Famers for ·
most of the decade, and is it possible? Was the dynamic duo injured
and unable to play? No, just the opposite. Aaron hit third or fourth
in 140-plus games every year in the 1960s. Mathews did close to the
same thing until 1964, when he split time hitting 41 times in the
second spot. Throw Felipe Alou into the top of the lineup, and still
the Milwaukee Braves, with their wonderful tomahawk uniforms,
still got scalped.

Although these Braves looked like the 1960s Giants of Mays/McCovey/
Cepeda, they had very little quality pitching, unlike the Giants. In 1963

Hall of Famer pitcher Warren Spahn led the staff with a 23–7 record … but he was forty-two years old. Former ace Lew Burdette was thirty-six years old. Surrounded by an average supporting cast, not even the likes of Aaron and Mathews could make up the difference.

WHERE'S THE BEEF?

Beef-O-Meter, 1960–1964

Score = Aaron 3, Mathews 3, Adcock 2 = Total 8

Score = Aaron 3, Mathews 3, Torre 2 = Total 8

Aaron and Mathews were Hall of Famers and three points. Joe Adcock was a very good slugger and was two points. Joe Torre was also a good hitter, later winning a batting title with the Cardinals, and was two points.

Torre came up as Adcock was leaving, and the Braves didn't enjoy the overlap of both for very long.

> "Well, it took me 17 years to get 3,000 hits in baseball,
> and I did it in one afternoon on the golf course."
> —Hank Aaron

Beef-O-Meter, 1965–1969

Aaron continued to dominate, however Mathews began to slip. Torre hit fourth in the order the most from 1964–1968, until he was traded for Orlando Cepeda, who hit fourth for the Braves in 1969. Behind Aaron and Torre during this period were Rico Carty, Tito Francona, and Clete Boyer. Only Carty was fit for the job.

Score = Aaron 3, Torre 2, Carty 2 = Total 7

Score = Aaron 3, Torre 2, Francona/Boyer/Others 0 = Total 5

ANALYSIS

With the "Screaming Brave" tomahawk jersey, combined with a navy blue hat supporting a red bill and the white "M" for Milwaukee on the front, the Braves had the coolest uniforms in the National League in the early 1960s. With Aaron, Mathews, and Adcock as their beef and legendary Warren Spahn on the mound, the Braves were a very exciting team to watch. In reality, the team's best years had come and gone. They would go nearly forty years from their world champion status in 1957 before they could claim another. That time would not come until Maddux, Smoltz, and Glavine ruled the mound during the nineties. Although they had outstanding middle hitting, including two of the greatest home run hitters in the game, the rest of the lineup and pitching wasn't enough. The Braves resembled the Giants of the sixties on paper when they peaked in the 1950s, being loaded with stars and good pitching. But by 1965, they had lost their luster in Milwaukee and left for Atlanta for the 1966 season.

JOE TORRE: NOT IN THE HALL?

Joe Torre will probably get into Cooperstown as a result of his managing, mainly in recognition of his success as the skipper of the New York Yankees. However, his numbers as a player merit consideration by themselves. He was a nine-time All Star with 252 career home runs and 1,185 RBI. His .297 lifetime average is supported by his league-leading .363 in 1971; it was that year that he also lead the league in hits with 230, RBI with 137, and total bases with 352. He was voted the NL MVP that year even though his team, the Cardinals, didn't make the playoffs. With 2,342 career hits, a Gold Glove in 1965, and finishing seven times in the MVP voting, Torre's credentials are very impressive for someone who spent much of his career as a catcher. Regardless of whether he is remembered as a player or manager, he still isn't in the Hall. "Say it ain't so, Joe!"

"I Must Be in the Front Row"

Bob Uecker is remembered by many different people for many different reasons. Most often it is his association with baseball. Whether it his longtime career as the Milwaukee Brewers announcer, the Miller Lite commercials of the 1970s, the three *Major League* films as the heavy-drinking Cleveland Indian announcer Harry Doyle, or his ninety-plus appearances doing his baseball comic routine on *The Tonight Show Starring Johnny Carson*, people recognize and enjoy Bob Uecker. What most people don't realize is that he was a major league player. Well, sort of ...

The Milwaukee Braves signed Uecker in 1956 right after her graduated from Technical High School in Milwaukee. He spent seven years in the minors before making his big league debut with the Braves on April 13, 1962. He spent 1962 and 1963 with Milwaukee before being traded to the Saint Louis Cardinals for the 1964 season. It was that season that he picked up a World Series ring as a backup catcher for Tim McCarver; however, he was the starting catcher on opening day. After another season in Saint Louis, they dealt him to the Phillies for 1966 and part of the 1967 season. After being traded to the Atlanta Braves during the 1967 season, Uecker's career came to an end. Nonetheless, his career numbers actually became part of and fueled his comic stick later in life. His lifetime .200 average with 13 career home runs and 74 RBI deserve a little more consideration than what Ueck is given. Yes, a career that ends with a .200 average is near the historical bottom for MLB players that played for seven seasons, but it was the 13 career home runs that gave him bragging rights. Of the 13 career home runs, 3 were hit off Hall of Famers. On May 5, 1965, he took Gaylord Perry deep in Saint Louis. As I listened in disbelief on my transistor radio the night of July 24, 1965, he took Sandy Koufax deep at Dodger Stadium. And finally, on April 29, 1966, in Chicago's Wrigley Field, Ferguson Jenkins fell victim to the Ueck's wrath. All three pitchers were Hall of Fame pitchers in their prime at the time. The really amazing thing is that all three homeruns were in succession for his career homers—and this despite being spread over nearly a year!

There was no end to Uecker's speed and prowess while on the base paths. In seven years in the majors, he *never* had a stolen base! By the same token, though, he was gunned down only three times. This was understood about Ueck, he toiled several years in the minors and had only one theft. That happened in 1959, while in the South Atlantic League on the Braves' Jacksonville single-A club. He never had a triple in the majors, either!

Although he was considered a decent defensive catcher, even the wheels came off that claim in 1967, his last year. Playing for the Phillies and Braves that season, Uecker appeared in fifty-nine games. He allowed twenty-five passed balls, which puts him on the all-time list for a single season; he combined that with nine errors. Contemporary player and Hall Famer Johnny Bench, who would set the standard for catchers defensively, had a whole season where he caught 121 games without even a single error; he had only 97 in his entire career while catching some 1,742 games.

As his on-field career came to an end, his off-field antics were just beginning. He had appearances on *Saturday Night Live*, the *Late Show with David Letterman*, and *The Tonight Show* with both Johnny Carson and Jay Leno. He appeared on *Studio 42* with Bob Costas, plus a host of other sports shows. His career in numerous 1970s television ads for Miller Lite became iconic. He had several small parts in several Hollywood pictures. From 1985–1990 he was George Owens in his own TV sitcom, *Mr. Belvedere*. He has been the color man for both ABC and NBC, including League Championship and World Series games. At one point Ueck was the ring announcer for a World Wrestling Federation "Wrestle Mania" event. Since 1971 he has been the announcer for the Milwaukee Brewers, and he received the Ford Frick Award in 2003 for his career in broadcasting. Whether he is honored by the Brewers with their dollar nosebleed, obstructed-view seats, or the new statue at the stadium, Uecker certainly parlayed an on-field lackluster career to an off-field dream come true.

The following quotes are attributed to Bob Uecker.

"The way to catch a knuckleball is to wait
until it stops rolling and pick it up!"

"In 1963 I was named minor league player of the
year. I was in my second season in the Bigs."

"I signed with the Milwaukee Braves for $3,000. That
bothered my dad at the time because he didn't have that
kind of dough. But he eventually scraped it up!"

"The highlight of my career? In 1967 with Saint Louis,
I walked with the bases loaded to drive in the winning
run in an intersquad game in Spring Training."

New York Mets

"Can't anybody here play this game?"
—Casey Stengel, Mets manager

O N Monday, September 15, 1969, the Mets beat the Saint Louis
Cardinals 4–3 in Saint Louis. The unusual thing about this game
is not that the New Yorkers won; it's how they did it. Steve Carlton,
the Cardinals pitcher, set a modern record that night by striking out
nineteen Mets. He lost as a result of a couple two-run homers by a .240
hitter named Ron Swoboda. The two homers brought Swoboda to nine
on the year. Some 13,086 fans watched that great pitching performance
that evening.

As destiny sometimes raises its head, it did for me that night, and for one
very unlucky fan in attendance. It seems that the stadium was attempting
to introduce Ron Santo Pizza to the crowd. This was supposed to be a
Chicago-style mini pizza. The staff asked if I would be willing to give
up selling peanuts that night and instead move about the stands selling
these small pizzas, and I agreed as a favor to my boss. As hard as it is to
believe, I was strapped to a fifty-pound metal box that had sharp corners
and a lit sterno in the bottom to keep the twenty or so pizzas warm. The
metal box was about two and half feet by two feet, and it was about two
and a half feet high. One can only imagine a young kid that was about

4'10" carrying this up and down the aisles all night. Well, the idea didn't catch on very well, and sales were slow. However, in the middle of the game a potential customer flagged me down. He was setting several seats down the aisle, but there was no one next to him, so I could walk right to his seat. After completing the transaction, I started to leave. At that exact moment an exciting play occurred down the right field line. As I moved to see the action, I swirled my heavy box around, nailing the head of the guy in the row below with the metal corner. He slumped like he had been hit by a Mohammad Ali right hook. After a short visit by the paramedics, the man seemed okay but a little dazed. If you are still out there, mister … sorry!

The 1960s decade began with a most unlikely world champion in the Pittsburgh Pirates. It would end with even a more unlikely world champion, a team not even in existence in 1960: the New York Mets.

The Mets began operations in 1962 in the old Polo Grounds. They were to be a replacement for the departed New York Giants and the Brooklyn Dodgers, for New York's National League fans who had been left without a team since 1958. Even their uniforms combined the colors of their predecessors, and they had even incorporated the Yankee pinstripes for the metropolitan appeal. The former Yankee legendary manager Casey Stengel was cast at the helm of the team to start of the '62 season. Despite a record of 40–120, the fans were hungry for NL baseball and adopted the amazing Mets.

From 1962 through 1968, the Mets finished ninth or tenth every year. Five times during that period they lost over 100 games in a season; the other two years they lost 95 and 89 games. In 1962 they gave up 948 runs while scoring 617. Most of the time (until 1968) they were outscored by over 200 runs a year! It would be a place over-the-hill stars like Richie Asburn, Duke Snider, and Ken Boyer would be dealt, to either finish or begin to play out their careers.

WHERE'S THE BEEF?

Beef-O-Meter, 1962–1964

In the early years, the Mets were so inept in the field that people felt like they were going to the circus rather than to see Major League Baseball. At the plate there was little difference. In 1962, the Mets had thirteen different players hitting in the three spot. To top that, they had seventeen different players hitting fifth! In 1964, Joe Christopher hit more than anyone else in the third and fourth spots. Despite having a good year in '64, he was a career .260 hitter with 29 home runs in eight seasons. He was joined in the five hole by Charlie Smith, a career .239 hitting machine. One of the fan favorites during this period was Ron Swoboda. A career .242 hitter with only 73 career home runs, Swoboda frequently hit fourth and fifth in the lineup. It would be 1969 before the Mets would even outscore the opposing teams for the year.

It's hard to evaluate a start-up franchise over the first three years, 1962–64. The Mets' main consistency during this period was Frank Thomas, former Pirates and Braves slugger who had 138 games in the fourth spot in 1962 (he had 34 home runs and 94 RBI that year), 76 times in the fourth spot, and 37 times in the five hole in 1963. Joe Christopher had a decent 1964 season, hitting .300 with 16 home runs and 76 RBI, however Thomas was gone by then.

Score = Thomas/Christopher 1 = Total 1, since no other consistency was present in other spots.

> "We was going to get you a birthday cake,
> but we figured you'd drop it!"
> —Casey Stengel, to first baseman Marv
> Throneberry on his defensive abilities

> "Blind people come to the park just to listen to him pitch."
> —Reggie Jackson, on Tom Seaver

Beef-0-Meter, 1965–1969

Ken Boyer (14 home runs, 61 RBI, .266 average) hit third and fourth in 1966 for the Mets. In 1967 he was gone, replaced by Tommy Davis (16 home runs 73 RBI .302 average). Both years Ed Kranepool, who had hit fourth in 1965, hit fifth behind the aging stars. By 1968 Davis was replaced by Cleon Jones for the next two years in the third and fourth spots. Swoboda and Kranepool were interchanged in the fifth spot during these seasons.

Score = Boyer/Davis 1, Kranepool 1 = Total 2

Score = Jones 1, Kranepool 1, Swoboda 0 = Total 2

It should be noted that even in their 1969 championship year, Ken Boswell (11 seasons with 31 career home runs and a .248 lifetime average) hit third in thirty games. Also, no points have been given for Swoboda, a career .242 hitter.

ANALYSIS

Early in the sixties, people used to say that the Mets winning a World Series would be about as probable as America putting a man on the moon. In 1969, both events happened! By 1969, the Mets had been transformed into a team that resembled the Los Angeles Dodgers. They were a team that would scratch out a run here and there, and shut out the opposing team. By 1968, the Mets had added Ken Holtzman, Tom Seaver, Nolan Ryan, and Tug McGraw (singer Tim McGraw's father) to the staff. That year, although they finished ninth, their record was twelve games better than the previous year. More important, that year they only gave up 499 runs and were outscored by only 26 runs for the entire season. In 1969, they gave up a few more runs at 541, but they scored more runs than in any other season since their existence, with 632. Finally it was that year that a team that had lost over a hundred games for five of the last seven years would win a hundred games in a season to become world champions!

HOUSTON COLT 45s/HOUSTON ASTROS

O NE OF THE ADVANTAGES TO growing up in the ST Louis area
during the sixties was the "Straight A" program sponsored by
the Cardinals. This was an annual program that the team provided to
the students in the area who achieved the highest grade point averages
during the quarter prior to the beginning of the season. Each student
was given a choice of three games, with two tickets to each game. As
you might guess, these were not prime seats—in fact, they were so high
up, in the upper deck of Busch Stadium, that you actually looked down
on the Saint Louis Arch! Well, not really, but the tickets did come with
an oxygen mask. Now, the opponents that you had to choose from rarely
would be a contender. This meant that the Mets and Astros would be
two of the teams that would be automatically included on the list. Every
once in a while, they might throw in the Giants or Braves. Nonetheless,
the Mets wound up winning the championship in 1969 and disappeared
from the list. Houston, on the other hand, probably is still a shoe-in to
make the list!

The Houston Colt 45s, along with the New York Mets, were the
National League's answer to expansion in 1962. For the first few years
Houston was not as bad as the Mets. They never lost a hundred games
in a season, though they did lose ninety or more games six of their first

seven years. This allowed them to finish eighth or worse every year from 1962 through the 1968 season. Like the Mets, their best year came in 1969, when the team posted an 81–81 record and finished fifth. Unlike the Mets, the Astros would take over forty years before going to the World Series. Furthermore, unlike the Mets, to this day they still have not won a world championship. Houston seemed to have better hitting than pitching during the decade. They had some stars in the form of Jim Wynn, Rusty Staub, and Joe Morgan. They consistently gave up more runs than they scored in every season until 1969, when they scored 676 and gave up 668. The 1960s set the tone for the lack of success for the Houston franchise.

WHERE'S THE BEEF?

Beef-O-Meter, 1962–1964

The lineup was mixed the first three years. In 1962 it was Roman Mejias, Norm Larker, and Carl Warwick. The next year it was Pete Runnels, Warwick, and Rusty Staub. For 1964 it was Joe Gaines, Walt Bond, and Bob Aspromonte. Of this bunch Staub was excellent and worth two points. Larker and Runnels were steady and were one point. So was Walt Bond, a budding star who would die of cancer in a couple years in his twenties.

Score = Runnels 1, Warwick 0, Staub 2 = Total 3

"I dunno. I never smoked any Astro Turf."
—Tug McGraw, on views of Astro Turf versus grass.

Beef-O-Meter, 1965–1969

Jim Wynn would hit third most of the time, followed by Rusty Staub. Sometimes they would be interchanged between the three and four spot, starting in 1968. Usually the fifth place hitter would be different each season. Eddie Mathews, practically done by this time, started fifty-eight games behind those two in 1967. The following year it was Dennis Menke. In 1966 Wynn hit third and Staub hit fifth. They were separated in the lineup when Dave Nicholson, a career .212 hitter, hit in the fourth spot. Although Wynn and Staub provided some punch to the lineup, there wasn't much else to go with them.

Score = Wynn 2, Staub 2, others 0 = Total 4

ANALYSIS

Houston started out as a market that would be similar to that of the Minnesota Twins or Pittsburgh Pirates. The media tends to overlook these franchises, and the players rarely receive the recognition that they deserve. Players from either coast seem to get the endorsements, the recognition, and election into baseball's Hall of Fame much easier than these types of markets. Unfortunately, the Houston franchise did not have the same success as some of the other expansion teams of their era. These overtones still continue fifty years later: the club has only one pennant and no world championships to its credit. In the sixties it looked as if the Mets would be the team with a not-so-bright future. Houston had Wynn, Staub, and Morgan, and it seemed to be maturing. The intrigue of the Astrodome, however, was more popular than the team; the Astros drew over two million the first year it opened. Houston was second in attendance and ninth in the standings that year. For ten consecutive years, a second-rate team drew over a million each season. Regardless, Houston had below average pitching and average hitting at best, so it was doomed for the seventies to be only average. It would not be until the 1980s, when former Met and Hall of Famer Nolan Ryan was acquired, that the franchise could enjoy better days.

AMERICAN LEAGUE WINS, REGULAR SEASON, 1960s

Baltimore Orioles.........911
New York Yankees.......887
Detroit Tigers...............882
Minnesota/Washington Twins...........862
Chicago White Sox.......852
Cleveland Indians..........783

Boston Red Sox............764
Kansas City/Oakland A's.....686
Los Angeles/California Angels.............685 (9 seasons)
Washington Senators.....607 (9 seasons)

INTRODUCTION TO THE AMERICAN LEAGUE

"Slump? I ain't in no slump. I just ain't hitting."
—Yogi Berra

On October 15, 1964, a worn-out Bob Gibson surrendered home runs to
Clete Boyer and Phil Linz in the top of the ninth inning of the seventh
game of the World Series. As he held on to get the final out in the midst of
a beautiful, warm autumn day in Saint Louis, little did anyone know that
the Yankee dynasty had just ended. Never again would the great Mickey
Mantle play in another World Series. In fact, as Gibson put the nail in the
Yankee coffin, it would be twelve years before the Yankees would play in
their next World Series game. It would begin a stretch of thirty-one seasons
and only two world championships for the New Yorkers! This juggernaut
had begun in 1923 with Babe Ruth. It had been passed on to Lou Gehrig in
the 1930s and then to Joe DiMaggio in the '40s. Through the 1950s Mickey
Mantle had carried the torch. It reeled off five consecutive pennants from
1960–64. On this day that all came to an end.

Going into the decade, the Yankees had won five world championships from 1949–1953. They had won the American League pennant every year from 1949–1958 with the exception of 1954, when the Indians won 111 games to capture the flag. They had won the pennant every year from 1949 through 1964, except in 1954 and 1959! Their players were household names. Never had baseball been so dominated for such a long period of time. But this was the sixties, and it was a decade of change in the world. So, too, was it for baseball.

Despite the Yankees' dominance of the first half of the decade, with five pennants and two world championships, it would be the Baltimore Orioles who would win more games than any other team in baseball during the 1960s. A middle of the lineup with two future Hall of Famers both named Robinson, one white and one black, would produce runs like a machine. They were supported by some of the greatest rotations and by Hall of Famer Jim Palmer, and the Os would begin their own run for dominance in the American League. It had been the best of times for the Yankees; but on October 15, 1964, it was about to become the worst of times.

DYNAMIC DUOS AND FEARSOME THREESOMES

During the 1960s, the American League teams were slaves to the National League when they met in the Summer All Star games. Nonetheless, they were not short on their 3-4-5 hitter threesomes. The best duo in baseball in the early 1960s was the combination of Roger Maris and Mickey Mantle. The "M & M Boys" hit an amazing 61 and 54 home runs, respectfully, in 1961. Maris would win the MVP Award in 1960 and 1961. Mantle, who had won the Triple Crown in 1956, would be a three-time MVP before hanging it up. This combination would approach the Ruth and Gehrig level. Add a Yogi Berra, Moose Skoworn, or Elston Howard in the fifth spot, and you had one of baseball's great middle lineups.

Another threesome during this time was the 1961–1963 Detroit Tigers' Al Kaline, Rocky Colavito, and Norm Cash. When the Yanks and the Tigers met during the season, the married men needed to be taken off the infield with those two ferocious lineups at work. Later in the decade, the Orioles' combination of Frank Robinson, Boog Powell, and Brooks Robinson would put opposing pitchers' ERAs into orbit.

Although, the threesomes were some of the best ever in history, the rest of the American League suffered to get the same 3-4 duos as the typical National League fan enjoyed. In Minnesota, however, there was Tony Oliva and Harmon Killebrew. Add Bobby Allison to this group, and it starts to look like some of the above threesome combos. Then there was Brooks Robinson and Jim Gentile in the early days for Baltimore. Tony Conigliaro and Yaz were second to none when it came to duos. Regardless, while the American guys may have had the edge on threesomes, the National Leaguers had the edge on duos.

As a kid in the day, growing up in a National League city, my opportunity to view these great hitters of the American League was limited to the World Series, the All Star game, or the Game of the Week. The World Series was always the Yankees. The All Star game tended to be dominated by Yankees. The Game of the Week usually rotated between leagues so that every other week it would be an American League game. When it was, it almost always involved the Yankees and somebody else. Combine that with a black-and-white television that had rabbit ears, and actually going to an NL game was quite different than watching the AL games on the tube. Like most kids, my family had no money to travel to other cities to see these other teams; they were trying to put food on the table. This limited exposure put more pressure on the radio in order to follow the American League. Nonetheless, through the Yankees, all teams were accessible.

NEW YORK YANKEES

T HE NEW YORK YANKEES ENTERED the 1960s embarrassed, after finishing in third place in the American League in 1959 with a record of 79–75. They would start 1960 with an average team age of twenty-eight years old, the exact age of Mickey Mantle. However, this was not a team that was inexperienced; many had been to World Series several times and had the rings to show for it. Mantle, though still a youth, already had won the Triple Crown in 1956 and was idolized by almost every young boy in America. The older Yankees like Berra and Ford had been part of the five consecutive world championship teams from 1949 through1953. A large percentage of the team had been on the most recent world championship team of 1958.

For the first five years of the decade, the Yankees would dominate not only the American League with five straight pennants, but all of baseball with two world titles; they won 505 regular-season games during this time. By 1964 they had won the pennant every year from 1949 to 1964 except twice. Rooting for the Yankees was like rooting for the sun to come up.

As tremendous as the first five years of the decade were for the Yankees, what happened on the back half is hard to believe. They would win only 382 games. Starting in 1965, they would have only one season where they would play above .500 for the remainder of the decade. The highest they would finish during this time was fifth place. In 1966 they would finish in last and would give up more runs than they would score. In 1967 they would finish next to last. By 1969 even the Mick was gone.

WHERE'S THE BEEF?

Beef-O-Meter, 1960–1964

In 1960 the Yankees were trying to find a consistent batting order that would indeed become iconic by the following year. In 1960, Mickey Mantle hit third 67 times and Roger Maris hit in that spot some 40 times. As to the cleanup spot, Maris hit there 65 times and Mantle hit there 46 times. They were followed in the five hole by Moose Skowron 68 times and Yogi Berra 34 times. As crazy as it seems, Maris led off 4 times and Mantle hit second in the lineup on 18 different occasions!

In 1961, the year Maris broke the home run record with 61 and Mantle hit 54 homers, the batting order became set. This was the year that New York set a season team record with 240 homeruns. That year Maris hit third 139 times and Mantle hit fourth 149 times .As hard as it is to believe, Maris, soon to be the all-time home run king, hit seventh in the lineup 10 times! Nonetheless, it would primarily be Maris followed by Mantle through the 1964 season and shortly thereafter. Each year they would see in the five hole Yogi Berra, Elston Howard, Joe Pepitone, Tom Tresh, or Moose Skowron. However, mainly Berra hit there, then Howard from 1961–1962. After that it was Pepitone and Tresh.

Score = Maris 3, Mantle 3, Berra 3, plus others to platoon 1 = Total 10

Score = Maris 3, Mantle 3, Howard, Pepitone, Tresh, or Skowron 2, plus others to platoon 1 = Total 9

As a special note, Maris is a three rating during this period and won MVP awards in 1960 and 1961. Elston Howard would also win an MVP in 1963; his numbers were offensively similar numbers to that of Skowron, Pepitone, and Tresh.

"Sure I played, did you think I was born seventy years old
sitting in a dugout trying to manage a guy like you?"
—Casey Stengel, responding to Mickey Mantle

"Baseball is 90 percent mental. The other half is physical."
—Yogi Berra

"The trouble is not that players have sex the night before a
game. It's that they stay out all night looking for it!"
—Casey Stengel

Beef-O-Meter, 1965–1969

Dr. Jekyll became Mr. Hyde for the Yankees as a team beginning in
1965. Mantle hit third most of the time from 1965–1968, but this was
not the Mickey Mantle of the 1950s and early 1960s; age and injuries
had taken their toll. Maris had slipped offensively, and opposing pitchers
had figured out Tresh. Kansas City no longer served as a trade supply
line for Yankee needs. Pepitone could not carry the torch. Jake Gibbs,
Phil Linz, Horace Clark, Steve Whitaker, and others were supposed to
replace Berra, Richardson, Ford, and Howard. The beef quickly became
lunch meat. The Yankee machine blew up like a cheap Chevy. Father
Time had had his way with the storied franchise. The Yankees were
terrible! In 1966, thirteen different players hit in the five hole. That same
year, Mantle hit .255 with 19 home runs and 46 RBI. In 1967, Steve
Whitaker hit fourth 21 times and fifth 64 times—his career numbers
were .230 with 24 home runs and 85 RBI. In 1968 Andy Kosko led the
way in the fifth hole by hitting there 60 times. In ten years Kosko was
a .236 with 73 home runs and 267 RBI. Then, when 1968 was over,
Mickey Mantle left the game.

Score = Mantle 2, Pepitone 1, everybody who hit fifth 0, = Total 3

ANALYSIS

It was hard for Yankee nation to witness one of the most dramatic
changes in baseball history as New York went from one the greatest

franchises in sports history to a level of obscurity that resembled that known only in minor league circles. How could this have happened? It appeared to resemble the sudden disaster of *Titanic* some fifty-plus years earlier. The strongest of strong sailed the great ocean one day and then hit an iceberg and settled at the bottom of the sea the next day. But was that the way it really happened? Did the Yankee ship have holes and leaks prior to 1965? What really took place here?

To get a handle on what and why things may have happened to Yankees, one must explore several possibilities and events that went unnoticed until the climactic end of their run. The first indication that there was a problem was during the 1959 season. The Yankees entered the season having won the pennant nine of the last ten years. They had rebounded from their 1957 World Series loss to Milwaukee to beat them in 1958 for the championship. This was a great Braves team with several Hall of Famers in their prime. With most everyone from that '58 team, the Yankees should have easily won the American League pennant the next year. They did not. In fact, they finished in third place, only four games over .500. Had they gotten too comfortable and too self-assured? Had they become overconfident as a result of their success?

Like a great boxer who had been knocked to the canvas, in 1960 the Yankees slugged their way back to the American League pennant and were heavy favorites in the World Series against the Pittsburgh Pirates. When it was over, Mantle sat at his locker and wept in disbelief that they had been beaten. Even the Pirate fans, who had watched their team be destroyed in some of the earlier games in the Series, were shocked.

Again, like a true champ, the Yankees dusted themselves off and won the pennant and the World Series by destroying the Cincinnati Reds in five games in 1961. In 1962, they repeated the process against Willie Mays' San Francisco Giants. However, had Bobby Richardson not leaped and grabbed Willie McCovey's line drive with men on base for the final out in Game 7, they would have lost that series.

Yankee confidence produced yet another pennant in 1963, but the Yanks were clobbered in four straight by the Dodgers and Sandy Koufax. However, again the Yankees got off the mat and rebounded to capture the American League flag in 1964. But like all great boxers, there are only so many comebacks to be had. The Yankees' legs had become wobbly, and they proceeded to lose to the Cardinals in seven games for the October championship.

Had all those championships of the past become an automatic expectation for everyone in New York? Did the Yanks become lackadaisical in their efforts? Did they grow bored with winning? Were they too confident, or could it have been something else?

While Mickey Mantle was the New York Yankees leader on the field, he was also the leader off the field. Mantle was unique; unlike his teammates, he could go to the plate half sober and hit the game-winning home run. He could stay out all night and have a perfect day at the plate the next day. Mantle was one of baseball's greatest natural talents. However, not even Mantle could endure that lifestyle forever. His last great season was 1964, when he was only thirty-two years old. He was done with baseball in 1968, when he was only thirty-six. Could this be why his off-field player buddies started to slow in their performance at about the same time? Could it have been that when Mantle began his decline, his teammates lost their protection and started to be exposed for their true talent? Had these been only average ballplayers that had been elevated by Mantle's greatness? Regardless of whatever one wants to believe, Mantle did have an impact both on and off the field.

Another possibility that may be considered is the cockiness of the front office. What ownership changes managers four times while winning five consecutive pennants? After the 1960 season, Casey Stengel was replaced by Ralph Houk. Houk was replaced for the 1964 season by Yogi Berra. Berra was replaced by Jonny Keane for 1965. In 1966, Keane was replaced by Houk. That's five manager changes from the end of 1960 to twenty games into the 1966 season! Who does that and doesn't expect it to impact the team on the field? Despite all those changes, the Yankees won five consecutive pennants, revealing that the players really had the talent and the power. With this power, the players were free to do as they wish. Why not? They were assured by the front office that the manager's job was only temporary!

Finally, after the 1960 World Series both manager Casey Stengel and GM George Weiss were let go. Casey took the hit as the series scapegoat for not starting Whitey Ford in Game 1. Had he done that, Ford could have pitched three times in the series, including the pivotal Game 7. Weiss, the inventor of the Yankee farm system and the GM during the Yankee championships from the late 1940s through 1960, was in the final year of his contract. As he left, he said that the Yankee dynasty was close to ending in a few years, as the talent from the minors had dried up. Interesting enough was that it had been Weiss who had created so many Yankee stars from their minor league system. Yet how could he have been the reason for their collapse and the lack of new talent? Weiss was often considered by many as a racial bigot. This, plus the fact that the Yankees were very slow to integrate blacks and Hispanics compared to other teams during the late 1940s to mid-1950s, put the team at a disadvantage. It was not until 1955 when Elston Howard became the first black on the Yankee roster. That was seven years after Jackie Robinson was introduced as a Dodger in 1947. By 1955, the other two New York teams, the Dodgers and Giants, had won pennants with their black stars. Additionally, many other teams had acquired star players from the Negro League with great success. This theory is consistent, because it was Weiss that traded off Billy Martin on a falsely accused brawl at the Copacabana and pointed out that he didn't have that Yankee look or act like a Yankee. Similar, to the Yankees, the Red Sox suffered for many years, and they were even further behind the Yankees in the area of integration.

Nonetheless, the Yankees' fall wasn't as sudden as many want to believe. It had actually begun in 1959, and the signs continued to show themselves several times over the next few years. Had Richardson not snagged McCovey's line drive in 1962, the Yankees would have lost four of the five World Series in the sixties. Had that happened, their fall could have been more predictable. Had the players not been so talented, the cover-up would have not gone unexposed so long. Had the winning not had gone on for so many decades, the gradual decay could have been more visible. However, like the Roman Empire, in the end, Father Time did have his way; he just went about it slowly and virtually unnoticed!

"They told me my services were no longer needed because they wanted to put in a youth program as an advance way to keep the club going. I'll never make the mistake of being 70 years old again!"
—Casey Stengel

"Whether you quit, retire or get fired ... it's time to go!"
—Casey Stengel

"UNLUCKIEST MAN" ON THE FACE OF THE EARTH: JOHNNY KEANE

On July 4, 1939, a dying Lou Gehrig stood before a somber crowd at Yankee Stadium and declared himself the "luckiest man on the face of the earth." After losing sixteen of the first twenty games of the 1966 season, Yankee manager Johnny Keane was fired as the skipper of the New York team. Keane had spent seventeen seasons as a manager in the Saint Louis Cardinal system before becoming a coach in 1959. He was promoted to manager in 1961 and led the Cardinals to a World Series victory over the Yankees in 1964. Immediately after the series victory, the Birds front office gave him a contract extension. He declined. The Yankees, whom he had just defeated, wanted him to manage their club for the 1965 season. On the surface it looked like a dream come true. The Yankees had just won the pennant every year, except two, from 1949–1964. New York was a much more impressive franchise than Saint Louis. Besides, the Cardinals' pennant drive had been extremely lucky due to the Phillies' collapse, as the Cards won the pennant on the last day of the season. The Yankee bench still had Maris, Mantle, Ford, Boyer, and Richardson, plus what looked to be other future stars.

What looked great on paper turned into a disaster. The Yankees were getting old quick, and the prospects were not what they'd appeared to be. They finished sixth in Keane's first year, 1965. After three weeks into the 1966 season, Keane was replaced with Ralph Houk. Keane, not the Yankee players, was the scapegoat. The New York decline continued, and the Yanks did not get back to the series again until 1976.

Had Keane stayed with the Cardinals, he would have probably had been the manager of the 1967 world champion club and the pennant-winning team of 1968. We will never know, and Johnny Keane died of a heart attack at fifty-five years old in November 1967. This was about a year and a half from the time he was fired as the Yankee manager, and that move to the aging Yankees made him one of the unluckiest men alive. Ironically, Gehrig lived nearly two years from the time of his speech, a little longer than when Keane realized his futile mistake in the spring of 1966!

> "The secret to managing is to keep the guys who hate
> you away from the guys who are undecided."
> —Casey Stengel

DETROIT TIGERS

A S A KID, I GOT to go to Detroit and see a game at Tiger Stadium. The two things I remember about that day were that the stadium was old and that Al Kaline owned right field. It was obvious he had grown up with the wall. Every great defensive ballplayer grew up with a wall. Whether it was the side of the house, the garage door, a retail outlet, or the school yard, there was a wall to throw the ball against, catch with your glove, and hone your defensive skills as a youngster. Hours upon hours were spent in this fashion when no other kids were available. For fly balls, you would throw the ball at the top half of the wall. For infield grounders, you would throw at the bottom half. Soon your imagination had you in the World Series, saving the day for your favorite team. If you were Roberto Clemente, your wall was in Puerto Rico. If you were Brooks Robinson, your wall was in Arkansas. Mine was in Cahokia, Illinois. All the greats had a wall. As I watch some of the present day ballplayers and see their defensive skills, I think that when they went to the wall, they took a can of spray paint rather than their ball glove.

The Detroit Tigers ended the 1950s as a team that had finished fifth or worse seven in an eight-team league in the last ten years. However, after a sixth-place 1960 finish, the Tigers would have a pretty good decade, finishing second three times and winning the World Series in 1968. The Tigers were a very good hitting club that featured an outstanding middle of the lineup. With Hall of Famer Al Kaline and Norm Cash (377 home runs, 1,103 RBI), either interchanged in the three and four spots, the Bengals would frequently have another power hitter in the mix. Nothing could have been more prevalent than in 1961, when the Tigers finished second to the Yankees. That year Kaline hit .324 with 19 home runs and 82 RBIs, and he led the league in doubles. He was supported by Cash, who hit .361 with 41 home runs and 132 RBIs, and Rocky Colavito's 42 home runs and 140 RBI. In addition to Colavito, the Cash-Kaline combo through the decade also featured Willie Horton, Jim Northrup, and Bill Freehan, who regularly joined the deadly combo in the fifth spot. Regardless of the great hitting, the Tigers would not see a big improvement until the pitching staff featured two outstanding hurlers in Mickey Lolich and Denny McClain. After two consecutive fourth place finishes in 1964 and 1965, the Tigers would finish the decade third, second, first, and second.

The Tigers made two outstanding trades prior to the 1960 season. One was Harvey Kuenn for Cleveland's Rocky Colavito. Kuenn had won the AL batting title as a Tiger in 1959 by hitting .353, but the Tigers wanted the Indians' Colavito, who had hit 42 home runs with 111 RBI that same year. While Kuenn would have a few more decent years, Colavito would hit 139 HRs and drive in 430 runs over the next four years. The second great acquisition for Detroit was getting Norm Cash for Steve Demeter. While Demeter would play only fifteen games in his entire career (and drive in only one run and hit .087), Cash would wind up with 377 career homers and 1,103 RBI.

WHERE'S THE BEEF?

Beef-O-Meter, 1960–1964

Score = Cash 2, Kaline/Hofer 3, Colavito 3 = Total 8

After trading Rocky Colavito to the Athletics for the 1964 season, the

Tigers welcomed Willie Horton to the Cash-Kaline combo for the remainder of the decade. Although Cash would hit primarily third followed by Kaline in the cleanup spot, the addition of Horton in the five hole (more permanently by 1965) and the emergence of Bill Freehan and Jim Northrup made the Tigers lineup a fearsome force.

> "All the fat guys watch me and say to their wives, 'See, there is a fat guy doing okay. Bring me another beer.'"
> —Mickey Lolich, Tigers pitcher

Beef-O-Meter, 1965–1969

Score = Cash 2, Kaline 3, Horton 2, plus 1 for Freehan and Northrup = Total 8

ANALYSIS

From 1936 to 1967, the Detroit Tigers went to the World Series only two times. One was the last year of World War Two, when not all of the former stars were back from the war. They did finish in second place eight times during those thirty-one years. When the Tigers won it all in 1968 against the Cardinals, there was much to celebrate. Since 1968, however, through the 2011 season the Tigers have been back to the series only two times in those forty-three years. This makes the Detroit teams of the sixties very important in their history. Blessed with some great hitting teams during this time, the Tigers seemed to usually fall one good pitcher short of a championship. Had it not been for the M & M Boys in 1961, that Detroit team, which won 101 games and finished second to the Yankees, could have easily won the pennant. So, too, could some of those other late sixties Tigers teams—had the Reds not traded Frank Robinson to the Orioles. Regardless, there was exciting baseball in Detroit in the sixties as the Tigers won 882 games to the Yankees' 887, but they won only one pennant while the New Yorkers captured the flag five times.

Bill Freehan: Not in the Hall?

While many people believe that Freehan doesn't belong in Cooperstown—having career numbers of 200 HR, 758 RBIs, 1591 hits, and a lifetime .262 batting average—there are others who beg to differ. This group points out that he was the best catcher in the AL for the 1960s. His eleven time All Star selections contributes to their thinking. He won five consecutive Gold Gloves from 1965–1969. He was also MVP runner up to Denny McClain in 1968 when he hit 25 HR with 84 RBIs and an OBP of .366. [he led the AL in HBP that year with 24]. Unfortunately, for him McClain was 31–6 that year. The previous year he was third in the voting to Carl Yastrzemski's Triple Crown year MVP and a great Harmon Killebrew year. Freehan won his lone championship ring in 1968 leading the Tiger's to a World Series win over the Cardinals in a seven game thriller. If the Hall is about the best of their era then Freehan was just that and belongs.

Boston Red Sox

JACK HAMILTON

PITCHER

ANGELS

On Friday, August 18, 1967, 31,027 Red Sox fans turned out at Fenway Park to watch their beloved Sox in the heat of a pennant race. Boston faced the Anaheim Angels. They won the first of a four-game series against the Angels by a score of 3–2. This race, which went down to the last day of the season, would find Boston on top and champions of the American League for first time in twenty-one years. This season would be referred to as "The Impossible Dream." But on this night, the dream became a nightmare for all of New England and the baseball world.

In the bottom of the fourth inning, a young twenty-two-year-old who seemed destined for Cooperstown dug in at the plate. Angel starter Jack Hamilton was on the hill. As the hitter, Tony Conigliaro, leaned in over the plate, Hamilton released an inside pitch that struck Conigliaro in the left cheek, shattering his face, dislocating his jaw, and doing severe damage to his left retina. With blood pouring from his noise, he was removed by a stretcher and taken to the hospital. He was gone for the season and out of baseball for eighteen months. Although he had a couple more productive seasons, his career would soon be over.

Tony Conigliaro was a native New Englander who had been signed by the Red Sox. When he was only nineteen years old in 1964, he became their starting left fielder. After hitting 24 home runs partway through the season, he broke his arm, which cost him rookie of the year honors. The next year he would lead the American League in home runs with 32. At the time, he became the second youngest person to reach 100 career home runs. His good looks, charm, and a willingness to stay after the game to sign autographs added to his talents on the field, and he became a favorite among all Sox fans.

Despite losing "Tony C," the Red Sox did go on to win the pennant before falling to the Saint Louis Cardinals in seven games that year. However, it was this one pitch that would continue the Red Sox curse, which had been in effect since they'd sold Babe Ruth nearly fifty years earlier to the hated Yankees. What may have happened with a healthy Conigliaro added to Carl Yastrzemski, George Scott, and Reggie Smith for the next several seasons, one can only imagine.

The Red Sox entered the decade of the 1960s as a very mediocre team. In the fifties they finished third four times, fourth four times, fifth once, and sixth once. Since 1918, they had been to the World Series only one time in 1946, and they lost to the Cardinals in seven games. By 1960 icon Ted Williams was over the hill, and it would be his last year. By 1967, the sixties had treated them harshly. From 1960–1966, they finished as follows: seventh, sixth, eighth, seventh, eighth, ninth, and ninth. But what gave them hope was that Yaz had become a superstar,

Jim Longborg was becoming an outstanding pitcher, and Reggie Smith and Rico Petrocelli were on their way to becoming stars.

WHERE'S THE BEEF?

Beef-O-Meter, 1960–1964

In 1960, Ted Williams retired. By 1961, Carl Yastrzemski became entrenched in the three hole of the Boston lineup for the rest of the decade. In five of the ten seasons of the sixties he hit third in at least 150 games. Frank Malzone usually hit fourth or fifth during the early sixties, until he was joined by Dick Stuart in 1963 for two seasons. Though this created a formidable core in the middle of the lineup, the Red Sox pitching managed to give up more runs than they could score each year from 1960–1964. Beyond possibly Earl Wilson and Bill Monbouquette, there were no household names that took the mound for Boston in the early sixties. The Green Monster became the target of all of the visiting clubs.

Score = Yastrzemski 3, Stuart 2, Malzone 1 = Total 6

Starting in 1964, with the rookie Tony Conigliaro (who hit second that year) added to a lineup featuring Yaz, Dick Stuart, Frank Malzone, and Lee Thomas, the Sox would be an offensive force for the balance of the decade. They traded away Stuart before the 1965 season. By 1966–1967 Conigliaro, George "Boomer" Scott, and Reggie Smith were added to Yaz's bat. The two scenarios below show the impact on the team from Conigliaro's injury.

> "A baseball game is simply a nervous breakdown
> divided into nine innings."
> —Earl Wilson, Red Sox pitcher

Beef-O-Meter, 1965–1969

Score = Yaz 3, Conigliaro 3, Scott/Smith 2, quality platoons 1 = Total 9

Score = Yaz 3, Smith 2, Scott/Harrelson 2 Total 7

ANALYSIS

The Boston Red Sox won 764 games during the 1960s. This was almost 150 games less than what the Baltimore Orioles, the leader of all of baseball. The Sox were a bad organization in the early to mid-sixties until the 1967 season. They had not been a very good organization since the early 1920s. It was this curse of the Bambino that lasted until a world championship victory in 2004, nearly ninety years later! But it must be remembered that since 1967, the Sox have been pretty good. It was that '67 team that got the organization back to the credibility that it had had at the beginning of the twentieth century.

YAZ!

It is one thing to be passed the torch as a rookie from an American legend like Ted Williams. It's another thing when your team finishes no better than sixth place in your first seven years, and yet you go out and play every day and put up Cooperstown numbers. But it is the "Impossible Dream" when you single-handedly carry a team that had finished in ninth place the two previous seasons and had lost the talented Conigliaro late in the season of a pennant drive, and you come within a game of a world championship.

No player in the sixties epitomized the meaning of leadership better than what Carl Yastrzemski did for the Boston Red Sox. Anointed with the responsibility to take over for the retired Williams, the unassuming Yastrzemski stepped into the icon's role and was the heart and soul of the Red Sox for over two decades. But it was the 1967 season that made Yaz a legend.

Going into that year, the Sox were expected to once again dwell near the bottom of the American League. To win the pennant seemed impossible. But this was the year of the impossible dream. In August of that year, the Sox found themselves in an unfamiliar position: a pennant race. However, half the American League was still in it. Then in a heartbeat, Tony Conigliaro was hit in the face by a Jack Hamilton pitch. With their great young star now gone for the season, the Red Sox felt like their chances were gone. Like a great fighter getting up off the mat and storming back, Yaz took over. Not only did he step up, but he told his teammates to get on his back, and he would carry them to the pennant. Yastrzemski did carry them, as he won the American MVP and the Triple Crown. On the season, Yaz hit .326 with 44 home runs and 121 RBI. When they need him the most, in the final two weeks of the season and with the pennant race at stake, Yaz went 23 for 44 (.513) with 5 homers and 16 RBI! Even in Game 7 of the World Series, with his team down 7–2 in the bottom of the ninth, Yaz led off with a single before being doubled up on Ken Harrelson's grounder.

Carl Yastrzemski would go on to be a first-ballot Hall of Famer. He would be an eighteen-time All Star and would win seven Gold Gloves. As of the 2011 season, he is the last player to win the Triple Crown. He hit 452 HR and drive in 1,844 during his career while getting 3,419 hits. But that October day, when Harrelson hit into a double play, the impossible dream was only one out from ending. It was as if the Cardinals knew they had to drive a stake in Yaz in order to kill the Sox. Ironic as it may seem, Yaz would lead his team to the 1975 World Series, and in the final game it would be Yaz who would make the final out on a fly ball to center. Then again, in 1978 in a one-game playoff against the Yankees (the Bucky Dent game), it would be Yaz that would pop to third to end the Red Sox season. By now all of baseball knew that to put an end to the Sox, you had to kill their soul … a man called Yaz!

CLEVELAND INDIANS

"I play for the Indians."
"Here in Cleveland? I didn't know they still had a team."
"Yup, we've got uniforms and everything. It's really *great!*" r
—*Major League*

MOST PEOPLE FEEL THAT THE drug revolution began in the late 1950s and early 1960s in California. It did not. It actually began in Cleveland, in November 1957, when the Cleveland Indians hired Frank Lane as their general manager. Lane was also known as "Frantic Frank," "Wheeler Dealer," or "Trader Lane," and the decisions that the front office made over the next three years at Lane's command led one to believe that the smoke coming out of the tee-pee in Cleveland wasn't because they had a log on the fire! After being run out of Saint Louis because he tried to trade the legendary Stan Musial—which owner Gussie Busch had to block—Cleveland decided Lane could help them as GM. The following transactions can be attributed to Frank Lane.

» June 15, 1958: Traded Roger Maris to Kansas City for Woody Held and Vic Power.

» December 15, 1959: Traded future Reds slugger Gordy

Coleman and starting pitcher Cal McLish to Cincinnati for Johnny Temple.

» April 12, 1960: Traded Norm Cash (who had been acquired on 12-6-1959) to Detroit for Steve Demeter, who would only play in 5 more games with 0 HR and 1 RBI in his career. Cash hit 377 HR and had 1,103 RBI in his career.

» April 17, 1960: Traded Rocky Colavito (one of the most popular Indians of all time, who would hit 139 HR and have 430 RBI over the next 4 years as a Tiger) for Harvey Kuenn, who would be shipped off to the Giants after one year.

» August 3, 1960: Traded Indian manager Joe Gordon for Detroit manager Jimmy Dykes.

» December 3, 1960: Traded Harvey Kuenn (who hit over .300 in 1960) for Willie Kirkland (career .240 hitter) and Johnny Antonelli (who was out of baseball the next year after going 0–4 with a 6.56 ERA in his only season).

In January 1961, the Indians fired Frank Lane. Amazingly, when Lane died in 1981, only one GM was there, and only at the request of Commissioner Bowie Kuhn. Lane deserved better, because he helped out many other GMs with his crazy trades.

Once Cleveland's front office had been trained properly by "The Wheeler," they continued the fiasco!

» November 27, 1962: Allowed Lou Piniella to be selected by the Senators in first year draft by not protecting him. Piniella had a nice career and started on some of the Yankee championships of the seventies.

» May 2, 1963: Traded Jim Perry (future two-time 20-game winner) for Jack Kralick.

» 1964: Sent Mike Cuellar (future star pitcher on the Orioles' championship teams) in a little disclosed and seemingly unkown transaction to Saint Louis. There was a lot of unknowns in Cleveland then!

»   June 15, 1964: Traded Mudcat Grant to Minnesota. (Minnesota would win the pennant in 1965, and Grant would go 21–7.)

»   January 20, 1965: Traded Tommie Agee (future 1966 ROY, two-time AS, two-time Gold Glover) and Tommy John (who would win another 286 games and was a legitimate Hall of Famer) to get back Rocky Colavito. (Colavito had one more good season left but had hit 173 HR since Cleveland traded him in 1960.)

»   January 20, 1965: Drafted future pitching star Joe Niekro (221 career wins) in the seventh round, but don't sign him.

»   March 10, 1966: Reacquired Lou Piniella.

»   October 15, 1968: Allowed Seattle Pilots to draft Lou Piniella and Tommy Harper by not protecting either one.

»   October 15, 1968: Traded starting pitcher Sonny Siebert (who won 45 games over next 3 seasons) to Boston.

»   November 21, 1969: Traded Jose Cardenal (1,913 career hits and several near .300 seasons with Chicago) to the Cardinals.

»   December 10, 1969: Traded Luis Tiant (229 career wins, three 20-win seasons in Boston) to the Red Sox.

I wonder if the movie *Major League*, where the front office deliberately tries to devalue the franchise in order to sell it by acquiring a group of no-name players, was written about the Tribe in the 1960s? After all, the team featured in the movie *was* the Cleveland Indians!

WHERE'S THE BEEF?

Beef-O-Meter, 1960–1964

The Cleveland batting order had the same consistency as their front office during the period from 1960–1964. Although Tito Francona and Willie Kirkland hit mainly in the third and fourth spots, there was still much chaos. In 1963, the Indians used the same full lineup only four times; eight different players hit in the third spot that year. An amazing eleven different batters hit in the five hole. The next year the Tribe had nine different players in the cleanup position, and they used twelve guys in the five spot. Abbott and Costello would really have had trouble with this lineup!

Score = Francona 1, Kirkland 1, no one in fifth slot = Total 2

Rocky Colavito returned to the Indians for the 1965 season, and he hit in the cleanup spot in all 162 games! That fact plus the emergence of Leon Wagner gave the Indians a nice one-two punch. Colavito rewarded the Tribe that year with a .287 average, 26 home runs, and 108 league-leading RBI. It was his last quality season. About the same time, Fred Whitfield added power and consistency in the fifth spot for three-plus years. Starting in 1967, it was back to the confusion.

> "Remember, fans, Tuesday is Die Hard Night. Free admission for anyone who was actually alive the last time the Indians won the pennant."
> —Bob Uecker as Harry Doyle, from *Major League*

Beef-O-Meter, 1965–1969

Score = Wagner 1, Colavito 2, Whitfield 1 = Total score 4

ANALYSIS

The Indians won 783 games in the 1960s. They finished third once, fourth once, fifth four times, sixth three times, and eighth once. This was an amazing performance considering the front office was a disaster. They have a long history of being an average franchise at best. They have only one world championship since 1920, when the great Tris Speaker roamed the outfield. That championship came in 1948, when they had Hall of Famers Bob Feller and Lou Boudreau.

The imagination could run wild had the Indians stayed pat with what they had come up through their organization in the sixties. Imagine a starting lineup of Roger Maris, Rocky Colavito, Norm Cash, Gordy Coleman, Tommie Agee, Lou Piniella, Jose Cardenal, and Tommy Harper, with a pitching staff of Sam McDowell, Sonny Siebert, Mike Cuellar, Joe Niekro, Mudcat Grant, Jim Perry, Luis Tiant, and Tommy John.

THE COLAVITO CURSE

The "Colavito Curse" involves the so-called curse that the Cleveland Indians have had since trading one of the most popular sports figures in Cleveland history, Rocky Colavito, to the Detroit Tigers in April 1960. Colavito was traded for the previous year's AL batting champion, Harvey Kuenn. Colavito went on to tear apart AL pitching before returning to Cleveland on January 20, 1965, after a one-year stop in Kansas City in 1964.

The curse is supposed to be because of that trade. In reality, this was nothing more than a continuation of GM Frank Lane's craziness, which had started a few years earlier and continued in the Cleveland front office after Lane's departure. Cleveland traded numerous future stars during this period. To claim one trade in particular caused the curse is ridiculous. When Colavito showed up in Detroit, he joined not only Al Kaline but Norm Cash, who was traded by Cleveland just five days earlier.

If there was a real curse, it was on Colavito himself. Despite being a consistent, premier AL slugger, he deserved better than being over the hill at a young thirty-two years old, and he was out of the game at thirty-four. Few players lose their skills at such a rapid pace. With any luck, he should have been able to play three or four more years and would have made it to Cooperstown as a sure bet. Not only was he repeatedly traded like yesterday's news, but he was traded in his prime. He never had the chance to play in a postseason game despite being one of the top players of his day.

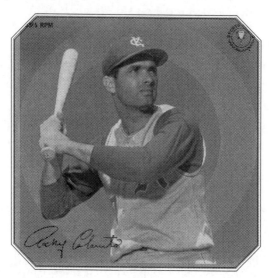

ROCKY COLAVITO: NOT IN THE HALL?

Colavito played much of his career for poor teams like Cleveland and Kansas City. At the time, these two clubs were consistently at or near the bottom of the American League. However, when in Detroit for a good Tiger team, Colavito flourished and produced gigantic numbers. He was a nine-time All Star, with six 100+ RBI seasons (1,159 career RBI), seven seasons of 30 + homers, three seasons of 40+ home runs, and 374 career home runs. The stats put this slugger in the company of many already in Cooperstown.

CHICAGO WHITE SOX

THE WHITE SOX FRANCHISE HAD been thrown into mediocrity since the Black Sox scandal of the 1919 World Series, and Chicago dwelled in the bottom half of the American League until the early 1950s. Starting in 1952 and through 1965, however, the Sox finished third or better in twelve of the next fourteen years; in 1957 and 1958, they finished second. In 1959, the "Go-Go Sox," as they were known, won the AL pennant before losing the World Series to the Dodgers four games to two. This was their first Series appearance since 1919, and it would be their last until 2005. They went from 1917 to 2005 without a World Series title—a stretch of 88 years!

As the Sox entered the 1960s, they were coming off and AL champion year. Unfortunately, the Yankees were still in their prime. The Sox would finish third to the Yankees in 1960, and in second place twice to the New Yorkers in both 1963 and 1964. Chicago would also be the runner-up again to the champion Minnesota Twins in 1965. In 1967 they went to the wire with three other teams to the last weekend of the season before finishing in fourth, three games back of Boston. From 1960 through 1967 the Sox won at least 83 games each year while never playing below .500 baseball.

A team based on pitching, speed, and defense, the White Sox won 852 games during the decade. This was a mere 35 games less than the Yankees over a ten-year period. Nonetheless, the Yankees won five pennants and two world championships, while the best Chicago could do was to play the bridesmaid three times.

WHERE'S THE BEEF?

Beef-O-Meter, 1960–1964

As good as the Chicago pitching was, the hitting was simply not there to support the efforts. In 1960, the 3-4-5 spots were most frequented by Minnie Minoso, Roy Sievers, and Sherm Lollar. But then in 1962, Jim Landis (career 93 home runs, 467 RBI, .247 average) was in the mix. Floyd Robinson and Pete Ward would team up in the middle starting in 1963. By 1964 the fifth hole was occupied by their shortstop Ron Hansen (.234, 106 homers over 15 years).

Score = Minoso 1, Sievers 2, Lollar 0 = Total 3

Score = Robinson 1, Ward 1, Hansen 0 = Total 2

> "Nellie was the toughest out for me. In twelve years, I struck
> him out once and I think the umpire blew the call!"
> —Yankee pitcher Whitey Ford, on Nellie Fox

Beef-O-Meter, 1965–1969

Floyd Robinson continued to be a force in the White Sox order, and he was joined by Pete Ward, who was also starting to put up decent numbers. Unfortunately, Ward hurt his back in a car accident in 1965 and would never be the same. Through the remainder of the decade, the Sox continued to attempt to bring in other over-the-hill players like Bill Skowron, Tommie Davis, and Ken Boyer to fill the middle gaps, but to no avail. By 1969, Bill Melton (.253 career), Ed Hermann (.240 career), and Buddy Bradford (.226 career) were the predominant 3-4-5 hitters in the Chicago lineup. The biggest bright spot for the Sox in the late sixties was the emergence of Tommie Agee, who would later be shipped off to the Mets and would become a world champion there in 1969.

Score = Robinson 1, Ward 1, no one else = Total 2

Score = Agee 1, Melton 0, Bradford/Herman 0= Total 1

ANALYSIS

On January 14, 1963, the White Sox traded Luis Aparicio to the Baltimore Orioles. In that deal, the Sox got Hoyt Wilhelm, Pete Ward, and Ron Hansen. The trade helped both teams, but the Sox got great relief help in Wilhelm, a decent shortstop in Hansen, and a middle of the order hitter in Ward for a few years to come. This trade probably kept the Sox in contention a little longer in the middle of the decade than what would have been possible otherwise.

Wilhelm, added to a starting pitching staff that featured Juan Pizarro, Tommie John, Joe Horlan, Gary Peters, John Buzhardt, and Ray Herbert made the Sox contenders during the sixties. This team, which searched constantly for a quality 3-4-5 lineup, resembled that of the Los Angeles Dodgers in the National League. Both played to a tune that featured great pitching, good defense, and very little offense. Drysdale and Koufax made the difference between three pennants and two world championships for the Dodgers, compared being a constant bridesmaid like Chicago.

OVERACHIEVERS OF THE AMERICAN LEAGUE

The Chicago White Sox won 852 games during the 1960s, 32 games less than the number won by the New York Yankees during the same time frame. That comes down to an average of 3.2 games per season. The Yankees won five pennants. If asked, the average fan could probably name many players on those Yankee teams. Ask the same fan to name some of the Sox players of the 1960s, and unless the fan was from the South Side of Chicago, that number he recalls would be greatly reduced. The Sox had very little beef during the decade, and Fox and Aparicio were both gone after the '62 season, so the number of total wins was quite impressive. The pitching staff may have gotten less credit than was deserved.

KANSAS CITY/OAKLAND ATHLETICS

ROGER MARIS, ENOS SLAUGHTER, HECTOR Lopez, Ralph Terry, Bob Cerv, Clete Boyer, Art Ditmar, Bobby Shantz, Ryne Duren, Bud Daley, and Tommy Lasorda—these players were all traded to the Yankees from the Kansas City Athletics in the late fifties and early sixties. All but one appeared on the great Yankee teams of that time and were a part of their championships. The only one that didn't was Tommy Lasorda, who still went on to Cooperstown for enshrinement.

One is hard pressed to find an organization worse than Cleveland during the late fifties and early sixties, but the thirteen seasons of hell that the Athletics had from 1955–1967 certainly are right up there. From 1960 through 1967, the A's finished last, ninth, ninth, eighth, last, seventh, and last. By 1968 they were on a Greyhound bound for Oakland. So bad

was the KC situation that in 1961 they had thirteen different players hitting third, thirteen different players hitting cleanup, and fifteen different players that hit fifth. They lost ninety-six games or more five times in the decade, and they lost a hundred or more three times!

On October 8, 1956, in Game 5 of the World Series against the Brooklyn Dodgers, Don Larsen, the Yankee starter, struck out Dale Long for the only perfect game in World Series history. On May 23, 1961, Larsen started in left field for the Athletics and went 0–4. He batted clean up! Excuse me, wasn't this the organization of the Hundred Thousand Dollar Infield, Jimmy Foxx, and Connie Mack? It is okay that Larsen hit fourth? He may have been the best choice that day !

WHERE'S THE BEEF?

Beef-O-Meter, 1960–1964

Norm Siebern, acquired from the Yankees, was the main cleanup hitter until "The Rock" Colavito came in 1964. The A's hit Jerry Lumpe (12-year career: 47 home runs, 454 RBI, .268 average) third most of the time during this period. The whole world hit fifth. In 1964 the A's featured a very powerful 3-4-5 order: Ray Charles, Rocky Colavito, and "Diamond Jim" Gentile. They finished last. Go figure!

Score = Lumpe 1, Siebern 2, Charles 1 = Total 4

Score = Charles 1, Colavito 3, Gentile 2 = Total 6

> "He'd give you the shirt off his back. Of course,
> he'd call a press conference to announce it."
> —Catfish Hunter, on Reggie Jackson

> "I go back to 1965 with Reggie, but I guess I don't
> go far enough to remember when he was shy!"
> —A's teammate Rick Monday, on Reggie Jackson

Beef-O-Meter, 1965–1969

In 1968, the Kansas City Athletics became the Oakland Athletics. The sixties trash of the American League would soon become the star of baseball in the early 1970s. In 1968, there was Rick Monday, Bert Campaneris, Joe Rudi, Catfish Hunter, Sal Bando, and of course Reggie Jackson. They went from tenth place to 82–80 in 1968. They were above .500 for the first time in forever! The next year, they finished second. Within three years, they would be world champs three consecutive times!

Score = Hershberger 0, Cater 1, no one else = Total 1

Score = Jackson 3, Bando 2, Cater/Monday 1 = Total 6

ANALYSIS

It is amazing that once the A's stopped their major trading efforts with New York, the Yankee dynasty began to fall apart. How ironic that once that happened, the Athletics started to become good. It also didn't hurt to bring up Catfish Hunter, Rick Monday, Sal Bando, Bert Campaneris, and Reggie Jackson within a couple of years from one another.

The A's won only 686 games in the 1960s, with several extra wins added to that number once in Oakland. Even with the elevated numbers, that is an average of only 68 wins per year. Given that most of the time they played 162-game season, and … well, you do the math. The A's played in an old ballpark, in a bad part of town, and at a time that the Yankees dominated baseball. However, Kansas City fans patience would win out. Within a couple of years, the team would be with a new ballpark, in a convenient location and with a brand-new team called the Royals. They would have a true hero in George Brett. They would win their division several times, and in 1985 they would defeat the Saint Louis Cardinals for their first world Championship.

THE CIRCUS IS COMING TO TOWN!

"I have discovered in twenty years of moving a ball
park, that the knowledge of the game is usually in
inverse proportion to the price of the seats."
—Bill Veeck, owner

Bill Veeck, who had owned several ball teams during his life, was considered one of the all-time showmen in baseball history. After all, he had been credited with the ivy being put on the walls at Wrigley Field. He had pinch hit Eddie Gaedel, a midget, during one of the Saint Louis Browns games in 1951. In addition, he had the disastrous idea of "Disco Demolition" in Chicago when he owned the White Sox. He was by no means short of ideas on trying to get fans to the ball park.

In 1960, Charlie Finley became owner of the Kansas City Athletics. That year the circus came to Kansas City, and Major League Baseball, for the next eight years. There was Charlie Finley, sandwiched between Veeck's decades of ownership and years of baseball fiascos. Like Veeck, Finley had been a successful businessman from Chicago. Unlike Veeck, he seemed to have so much craziness in such a short period of time in Kansas City that he must have assumed his time on Earth was limited. As hard as it is to believe, Finley's list of ideas is so long that to cover all of them would be a book in itself.

From 1960 to 1967, Finley's Kansas City years can be highlighted as follows.

1. In 1961, he hired new manager Hank Bauer, who was playing right field at the time, over the PA system, asking him to come to the dugout and take over.

2. He changed the team logo in 1962 from the famous Athletic elephant to the A's.

3. That same year he introduced sleeveless jerseys.

4. In 1963 he changed the red, white, and blue colors of the

uniforms to gold and yellow. It would not be until 1966 that they would add white shoes to the dress.

5. In 1964, he paid the largest sum ever paid to a rock group, to get the Beetles to perform at Municipal Stadium.

6. On September 8, 1965, he had Bert Campaneris Day. This promotion had All Star Campaneris starting at shortstop, his usual position, and then moving to the other eight positions throughout the game. The end result was Campy going to the hospital for X-rays after a collision, when he tried to block the plate on Ed Kirkpatrick of the Angels while catching. Though similar in height, Kirkpatrick had at least thirty pounds on Campaneris.

7. A few weeks later, on September 25, Finley had fifty-nine-year-old Satchel Paige as the starter against the Red Sox. Paige pitched three scoreless innings and set down the last seven in a row to end his brief time out of retirement.

8. Missouri Governor Warren Hearnes gave him a mule, which he later named Charlie-O and which became the team mascot, to symbolize the "Missouri Mule" concept. Not enough to just accept the gift, Finley to it to cocktail parties, on the road to other stadiums (while keeping it in the club's road hotel), and to press conferences. He even had relief pitchers of the A's brought in on it during the games in KC.

9. Other promotional games included fireworks displays, cow milking, and greased pig contests.

10. Beyond the outfield walls were a zoo and a shepherd tending goats and sheep.

11. Then there was Harvey. This was the name of the mechanical rabbit installed to bring new balls to the home plate umpire.

12. To further assist the home plate ump was "Little Blowhard," a wind-blowing device to blow away the dirt from home plate.

13. Ball girls were hired for the first time in major league baseball to assist during the games, including one that was a former Miss USA.

14. Finley encouraged the league to experiment with orange baseballs during exhibition games.

15. Sometimes relief pitchers were brought in from the bullpen in yellow cabs.

16. He tried to change the dimensions of the outfield walls to reflect that of Yankee Stadium's short right field wall, which he contended led to all those Yankee championships. This was outlawed by the league. In turn, he painted an area to reflect the Yankee wall and had the PA announcer comment when he thought that it would have been a homerun in Yankee Stadium.

17. He wanted to put a statute in center field of the legendary Athletics manager Connie Mack.

18. Groundskeepers with space suits raked the infield and dusted the bases between innings.

19. Helium balloons with free game tickets attached were launched from Municipal Stadium, destined to land all over the Kansas City metro area.

20. He traded home run–hitting stars like Jim Gentile and Rocky Colavito when he determined a forty-foot fence he recently constructed in the outfield would help the Kansas City pitching staff and reduce the hitters' home run ability.

21. He created some crazy story about fishing to give pitcher Jim Hunter the nickname of Catfish.

22. He tried moving the team to California, Dallas, Atlanta, and Louisville during his tenure.

The list goes on and on. Despite these efforts, the A's kept losing, and in 1965 they drew a mere 528,344 to an old minor league, converted ball park in a bad part of town.

It is amazing that one man could come up with so many bad ideas that were disliked by both the fans and players in such a short time frame. Growing up a mere four hours away on the other side of the state of Missouri, in Saint Louis, with Hall of Famers and pennants and world championships, I had no idea this was even possible. Just think: where could you have gone and seen a major league game, visit the zoo, and watch the circus, all at the same time? Thanks, Charlie, for leaving Chicago and not stopping in Saint Louis on your way to Kansas City!

MINNESOTA TWINS

THE MINNESOTA TWINS DID NOT start the decade as the Minnesota Twins; they started as the hapless Washington Senators, a team based in Washington DC where the highlight of the season would be when the president of the United States would throw out the first ball on opening day. After that, it was lights out! "First in war, first in peace, last in the American League" was a very appropriate saying for the Senators approaching the 1960's.

In 1961, the former Senators became the Minnesota Twins. The 1960 Senators finished fifth in the standings. The American League then awarded the DC area a "new" Washington Senators franchise that would replace the leaving Senators. The new Twins, however, would finish seventh in 1961. In Minnesota, the

Twins increased attendance that year over their previous Washington association by 500,000, to 1.2 million. By 1963 they would be first in attendance despite a third-place finish. Minnesota loved their Twins.

In 1961, the middle of the twins order featured Harmon Killebrew, Bob Allison, and Jim Lemon. All three hit 25-plus home runs and had an average around .250–260 each year. Each would also either lead or challenge for the lead league in strikeouts. Eventually Lemon would go, but Killebrew and Allison would remain throughout most of the decade. Although the Twins would be competitive in 1962 and 1963, finishing second and third, respectfully, it wasn't until Tony Oliva became a part of the order starting in 1964 that the Twins would win the pennant the next year and finish first in their division in 1969, as well as place second in 1966 and 1967 (one game back of Boston).

WHERE'S THE BEEF?

Beef-O-Meter, 1960–1964

Killebrew and Allison were the one-two punch for the Twins during the early years of the decade. In 1960 and 1961 they were joined by Jim Lemon. In 1962 Lemon was replaced by Rich Rollins, a somewhat power hitter with a .250 average. In 1963, Rollins was moved out of the three hole, and Earl Battey would hit fifth behind Killebrew and Allison. In 1964, Tony Oliva would win rookie of the year and would hit third in front of Killebrew and Allison.

Score = Killebrew 3, Allison 2, Lemon/Rollins/Battey 1 = Total 6

Score = Oliva 3, Killebrew 3, Allison 2 = Total 8

> "He can knock the ball out of any park, including Yellowstone."
> —Orioles manager Paul Richards, on Harmon Killebrew

Beef-O-Meter, 1965–1969

The last half of the decade featured Oliva and Killebrew, and then

Allison (who started to slide) or Jimmy Hall or Don Mincher taking on the five hole. However, in 1967 the top of the lineup featured future Hall of Famer Rod Carew, who hit .328 that year. It was the hitting artists Carew and Oliva getting on base that allowed Killebrew to have a monster season in 1969, when he had 49 homers, 140 RBI, and a league-leading 145 walks as Minnesota won the division.

Score = Oliva 3, Killebrew 3, Mincher/Hall/Reese 1 = Total 7

ANALYSIS

The move by the Senators franchise in 1961 proved to be excellent. The Twins played well and drew even better. During the 1960s, the team had two first-place and three second-place finishes. The organization made very few trades and preferred to bring up talent like Carew, Oliva, and Jim Kaat. Nonetheless, two trades worked out very well. On April 4, 1960, the Twins traded power-hitting Roy Sievers (who would still have a couple more good years) for Earl Battey and Don Mincher, plus $150,000. Both Mincher and Battey would be Twin starters through most of the decade. The other trade was on June 15, 1964. The Twins traded George Banks and Lee Stange for Jim "Mudcat" Grant. Grant would go 21–7 in 1965 to help Minnesota win the pennant. He would be 50–35 through his years as a Twin.

The years in Washington had gone downhill since the great Walter Johnson. This was a franchise that even had Harmon Killebrew lead off a game in 1961! (Killebrew had 19 stolen bases in a twenty-two-year career, and he was caught stealing 18 times. He also had a lifetime .256 average and hit 573 home runs. None of these were valid reasons for him to lead off.) Once in Minnesota, however, the franchise stabilized with Oliva, Killebrew, and Allison. In fact in 1962, when the Twins finished second, they had the same starting lineup an amazing seventy times! It was these factors that resulted in the franchise winning 862 games in the decade, a mere five less than the New York Yankees during that same period.

Tony Oliva: Not in the Hall?

Tony Oliva was a hitting machine. He was rookie of the year in 1964, the year he won his first of three batting titles. He led the league in hits on five occasions. He was an eight-time All Star and had a .304 lifetime batting average. Throw in a Gold Glove, and Oliva certainly deserves a tier-three Hall of Fame enshrinement. Had injuries not plagued him through most of his career, his number might have been unbelievable.

Baltimore Orioles

Two dates within nine months of each other took the Baltimore Orioles to the World Series four times in the next six years. The first date was on October 9, 1965, when all of baseball was changed, as the Cincinnati Reds postponed their future by trading Frank Robinson to the O's for Jack Baldschun, Dick Simpson, and Milt Pappas. Then on June 6, 1967, during the amateur draft, Baltimore selected Bobby Grich, Davey Johnson, and Don Baylor. Up until this time, the team that would win more games that decade than any other team in baseball had struggled with a second-place finish in 1960, followed by third in '61, seventh in '62, fourth in '63, and third in '65.

With the acquisition of Frank Robinson, the O's immediately became world champs in 1966. After a sixth-place finish the next year, they bounced back to second place for 1968 and won the pennant with a 109–53 in 1969. In the early part of the 1960s, the team had Brooks Robinson and Jim Gentile as the middle of the lineup. But in 1962, Boog Powell started to be worked into the middle of order. With Powell and the two Robinsons, the O's became an offensive machine during the last half of the 1960s. It was exactly what the doctor ordered to go with their great pitching, featuring the likes of Hall of Famer Jim Palmer, Mike Cuellar, and Dave McNally.

WHERE'S THE BEEF?

Beef-O-Meter, 1960–1964

The Orioles were blessed with some great arms in the early sixties: there was Chuck Estrada, Steve Barber, Milt Pappas, Wally Bunker, and Robin Roberts, just to name a few. However, the offense could not support the pitching to make the O's a champ. Jim Gentile, who was acquired in a trade in late 1959, was a power hitter. His partner in the middle of the lineup, Brooks Robinson, was known more for his defensive skills than his hitting. Although competitive, the O's need more to win championships.

Score = B. Robinson 2, Gentile 2, Woodling/Brandt/Triandos 1 = Total 5

Score = B. Robinson 2, Gentile 2, Powell 2 = Total 6

> "I don't see why you reporters keep confusing Brooks Robinson
> and me. Can't you see that we wear different numbers?"
> —Frank Robinson

Beef-O-Meter, 1965–1969

Things came together for Baltimore during the second half of the sixties. Not only was Boog Powell becoming a major force, but Frank Robinson came over from the National League and immediately won the Triple Crown for the O's. In 1966 they used the same starting lineup some thirty-two times! The timing was perfect because the Baltimore pitching staff was better than ever, one of the best in baseball.

Score = F. Robinson 3, B. Robinson 2, Powell 3 = Total 8

ANALYSIS

The Baltimore Orioles won 911 regular season games during the decade, more than any other team in baseball. Clearly the Frank Robinson trade changed the balance of power in the American League, but it also meant that the Cincinnati Reds would go without his services at a crucial time when they were adding several of their future Hall of Famers. It potentially cost the Reds a couple of pennants. Although Robinson's contributions to the O's cannot be overstated, Baltimore had some other great players during this time. It would be a nice run for the Orioles for years to come. Not only did they have a great team, but they had a Hall of Fame manager in Earl Weaver.

PRESCILLA PARIS

In 1966 the Orioles played the Dodgers in the World Series. In 1966, I was in the sixth grade. In 1966, Prescilla Paris, a scrawny little girl with round glasses and bad hair, was in my class. At the time, it was not uncommon to have the same group of kids together year after year until junior high. The problem here was Prescilla. You see, she was a preacher's kid, and we all know how that works out: they either grow up pointing out everyone's mistakes—your obvious trip to an eternal damnation in hell—or they later show up on the Internet in *Girls Gone Wild*! Prescilla was the former. Many kids over the years had felt the teachers' wrath through this informant named Prescilla. If you picked your nose, she told. If you passed a note in class, she told. If you used a bad word, she told. If you happened to gaze at a girl's shirt, she told. If you fell asleep in class, she told. If you copied—you got it, she told. It was so bad that on the first day of school, everyone let Prescilla pick her desk first. After her choice, everyone else found a desk on the *other* side of the room. This mad scramble for an empty desk even resulted in an occasional fist fight. It was that bad.

When the World Series began that year, my time was up, and I was in Prescilla's barrel again. It started as I carefully tried to conceal my transistor radio and plug the tiny earphone into my ear, to hear the game that day. I had taken great strides to hide the attaching chord. The kids around me were cool about it because they wanted a constant update on the score of the game. The whole thing went well—until the fifth inning, when Prescilla caught on. The next thing I knew, not only was I not listening to the game, but I was now sitting in the principal's office awaiting my sentence.

Prescilla continued her moral judgment on me and my classmates, until about two weeks before school ended. However, it was that day in May when Prescilla's turn in the barrel came: her "sister" came to town.

The girls at that age had begun to develop to prepare for their journey to womanhood, and Mrs. Trost, the eighty-year-old teacher, had had a private meeting of girls about the subject. When this event happened, they were instructed to get up quietly, get out of their chair, nod at her, and go to the bathroom to take care of the situation. The boys were told that if they *ever* said anything, life as they knew it was over!

I must have been born with a little Rodney Dangerfield in me, or at least with some revengeful desires. As Prescilla got up from her seat, walked slowly down the aisle, and received the nod from Mrs. Trost, my years of hell from this Olive Oyl–looking monster got the best of me. I shouted, "Hey, where are you going?" A sense of relief came over me. This demon who had cost me the World Series and my transistor radio the previous fall was cast into a total embarrassment rarely known to the female gender! The class went wild—but so did Mrs. Trost, who grabbed me by the ear and escorted me down the hall to the principal's office. This was to be one for the ages; they even called in the male gym teacher to make sure the swats were hard enough. I must have written on the chalkboard over ten thousand times the last two weeks of the year, during my lunch hour and breaks while my classmates played outside in the beautiful spring weather. Somehow, I still was allowed to graduate to the seventh grade.

As for Prescilla, she was absent the rest of that year. I think her family moved that summer. I wonder if she has been happy living out her secluded life somewhere in the Himalayas, serving the needs of a group of Buddhist monks? I heard the scenery is wonderful there.

Los Angeles Angels

THE ANGELS CAME INTO EXISTENCE in 1961 as the American League expanded to ten teams. They played their first year in Wrigley Field (named after chewing gum founder) in south Los Angeles. It had been a minor league park since 1925, with a maximum seating capacity of 20,457. The power alleys were equal in both left-center and right–center, at 345 feet. Films like *Pride of the Yankees, Angels in the Outfield*, and *Damn Yankees* had been filmed there; television shows like *The Munsters* and *The Twilight Zone* had shot there as well. It was the park used in the popular baseball show *Home Run Derby* in the early 1960s. However, it would be the home for the Angels for only one season. It was demolished in 1966.

The Angels had been formed from the December 1960 draft. In that draft they acquired future six-time All Star Jim Fregosi. On December 14, 1960, they traded for future twenty-game winner Dean Chance. In early April 1961, they traded Lou Johnson for Leon Wagner. It was these transactions that made the Angels semi-competitive through the 1960s. They won 685 games over their first nine years 1961–1969; this projects to a ten-year decade of 761 games. That rate is higher than the new Washington Senators and Kansas City Athletics. That projected number of wins is only three wins less than the Boston Red Sox' 764 for the decade!

WHERE'S THE BEEF?

Beef-O-Meter, 1961–1964

The Angels were a team that struggled through the decade in the middle of the lineup. The pitching was decent but not great. From time to time, Los Angeles would attempt to beef up the lineup with an aging semi star. Players like Ted Kluszewski, Joe Adcock, and Norm Siebern were used in the cleanup spot, without much success. Leon Wagner had some good years. Lee Thomas hit 24 home runs with 70 RBI and a .284 average in 1961, and in 1962 he hit 26 homers with 104 RBI and a .290 average. Everybody else hit fifth, including Buck Rodgers (.232 average, 31 home runs in his career).

Score = Wagner 2, Thomas 1, fifth spot 0 = Total 3

By 1964, Jim Fregosi became established in the three spot. Though a good player, Fregosi was probably better suited hitting second (he hit there primarily in 1968) or in the leadoff spot. In, 1967 the Angels added Don Mincher from the Twins to be the cleanup hitter. Rick Reichardt would hit in the middle of the lineup interchangeably during this time

> " I heard that actors start working at six o'clock in the morning. That sort of soured me on the whole thing."
> —Angel's pitcher and well known play boy Bo Belinsky.

1965–1969 Beef-O-Meter

Score = Fregosi 1, Mincher 1, Reichardt 1 = Total 3

ANALYSIS

The Los Angeles Angels, who were created by a draft, began their franchise in 1961 and were owned by cowboy actor Gene Autry. They played in an old, minor league ball park used for filming movies and TV shows that could barely seat 20 000. The next year they would play home games in the park of their cross-town attendance rival, the Dodgers, in Dodger Stadium until 1966, when their new stadium in Anaheim was ready. By 1965, they changed their name and were known as the California Angels. Despite all this, the Angels had a pretty good decade. They finished third twice, fifth twice, and had a sixth-place season in their first nine years. Although they finished last in attendance their inaugural year (primarily due to the constraints of Wrigley Field), they would lead the American League in attendance in 1966 when they opened their new ball park in Anaheim, despite a sixth-place finish.

In 1961, they had five players who hit over 20 home runs—again a result of the 345-foot power alleys. Nonetheless, it would be the lack of power and hitting that would cause the Angels their woes. As late as 1965, they still would have fifteen different players hitting in the five hole. In 1967, they were in the pennant race for most of the season before falling seven and a half games back and finishing in fifth. Their record was 84–77. This was an amazing record and accomplishment because they were outscored by 21 runs over the entire season! Despite overcoming many obstacles early on in the 1960s, it would be over forty years before they would ever be seen in a World Series game.

OVERACHIEVERS, TOO!

Another impressive overachiever certainly was the Los Angeles Angels. Starting in 1961 as an expansion team, the Angels won 685 games over a nine-year period. This is only one game less than Kansas City's 686, who played all ten years of the decade and went in as an established team from the 1950s. It would be several years before the Angels played in their own home park. They, too, had little to no beef, yet they won 78 games more than the new Senators, who started as an expansion team in 1961.

WASHINGTON SENATORS

W ASHINGTON FANS HAD A LONG history with their baseball team by the time they packed up and moved to Texas after the 1971 season. Since 1901, fans had only seen one world championship. This dated back to 1924, when baseball icon Walter Johnson was on the hill. Although they won two other pennants, the team had dwelled near the bottom of the American League standings year after year. They were known as the Nationals until officially becoming the Senators in 1956. After years of losing seasons, owners were tired of the poor attendance and left Washington in 1961 to become the Minnesota Twins. Baseball wanted a team in the nation's capital, and it held an expansion draft in 1960 to create a new ball club in DC. Even though the names on the roster had been changed, fans were in for another decade of debacle. These new Senators would lose a hundred games or more from 1961 to 1964. In seven of the first eight seasons, they would finish no better than eighth place, and even then it was only a sixth-place finish in 1967. In 1963, they lost 106 games and were outscored by the opposition for the season by 234 runs! Of course they finished last. Attendance was always at or near the bottom of the American League. There would be a few stars beside Frank Howard and Ted Williams, the latter who became the manager for the 1969 season. It was under Williams that they had their only respectable season, with an 86–76 record, finishing fourth out of six teams in their division in the AL East.

The sad part about the situation is that after years of fans suffering, when the team left for Minnesota, many of those same players would take the Twins to the World Series in 1965. Already on the roster were Harmon Killebrew, Bob Allison, Zolio Versalles, Jim Kaat, Don Mincher and Earl Battey. It is little wonder that the last home game played by the Senators in 1971 was forfeited with them leading with one out left in the ninth, when frustrated fans poured onto the field. Whether you call them the Senators or the Nationals, the fans in DC have not had a World Series since the 1920s.

WHERE'S THE BEEF?

Beef-O-Meter, 1961–1964

During this time the Senators were just getting started. Frank Howard had not arrived from Los Angeles as of yet. They did have some pop from Chuck Hinton and Don Lock. Lock would average about .250, and during the '63 and '64 seasons he hit 27 and 28 home runs while driving in 82 and 80 runs, respectively. There would be several others in the middle with little consistency. During this time Washington would be outscored by nearly 150 or more runs per season; they would lose 100 games or more each of these seasons.

Score = Hinton 1, Lock 1 = Total 2

> "Baseball is the only field of endeavor where a man can succeed
> three times out of ten and be considered a good performer."
> —Ted Williams

Beef-O-Meter, 1965–1969

In 1965, slugging Frank Howard was added to the Senators lineup. Later on, Mike Epstein would be coupled with Howard to give them a little more punch. Regardless, the Nats still continued to struggle until their only season above .500, in 1969.

Score = Howard 2, Epstein 1, everybody else 0 = Total 3

ANALYSIS

There is not much to analyze about the 1960s Washington Senators. They won only 607 games in 9 years during the decade. That extrapolates out to an average of 67 wins and 95 losses per season. However it is analyzed, it's terrible. What a bad time to have a team forty miles down the road in the form of the Baltimore Orioles, stealing your fan base because they won more games in the decade than any other team in baseball. To add insult to injury, the players and the franchise that moved to Minnesota would win a pennant within four years and only lose 25 more games than the New York Yankees did during the entire decade. There were times Washington fans rejoiced, when they only finished 25 games behind the Yankees in a *season*!

There were tons of dignitaries and celebrities that threw out opening day pitches in Washington. Eleven presidents from 1901–1971 threw out baseballs to open the season there. Ted Williams even became the manager in 1969 until they left for Texas after the 1971 season. One can only imagine the conversations that Williams, the greatest hitter that ever lived, had with a bunch of career .240 hitters. I remember a television show that interviewed the players during this time. They said that Ted told them that if they wanted to hit a ground ball, then hit the top half of the ball! If they wanted to hit a fly ball hit, they should hit the bottom half of the ball. As if the Senators players could hope to control their hits like that!

WORST IN THE AMERICAN LEAGUE

The National league had the Mets and the Astros. The American League had the Senators and the A's as the league's doormat. Washington struggled each year to stay out of the basement of the American League and really never had a solid 3-4-5 combo. They struggled to have even a 3-4 combo. Kansas City would be faced with the same problem. When the A's moved to Oakland and began to bring up a wealth of talent, things slowly began to change for them. The two best teams, the Yankees and Baltimore, clearly had a solid middle of the order. In addition, these two clubs had some pretty good pitching. Neither the A's nor the Nats could boast of that for several of the first years of the sixties.

The A's averaged 68.6 wins per year over ten years. The Senators averaged 67.4 over nine years. At that pace they would average to win nearly 24 games a year less than the Orioles, the winningest team in the American League!

Conclusion
The Baseball of the 1960s...
The Way It Was!

Outstanding Games of the Decade

R ECENTLY, ONE OF THE GREATEST finds in baseball history occurred when a full-length film of the final game of the 1960 World Series, between the New York Yankees and Pittsburgh Pirates, was discovered, and it soon became available for sale to the public. Without a doubt this had to be the greatest game of the 1960s. This was as good as the Bobby Thompson game of ten years earlier. Prior to 1969 there was no postseason play unless two teams tied for the pennant at the end of the regular season. This format made the World Series everything. The underdog Pirates beat the Goliath Yankees 10–9 in the seventh game of the World Series in the bottom of the ninth with a walk-off home run. Even Hollywood would have not bought a script like that!

The only pennant playoff in the 1960s happened in the fall of 1962, when the Giants and the Dodgers finished the season in a tie for the pennant. In the three-game playoff that followed, the teams split the first two. This set up a deciding Game 3. Going into the top of the ninth in Los Angeles, the Dodgers held a 4–3 lead. The Giants would get four runs in the ninth and win the pennant by a score of 7–4.

Shortly after the dramatic comeback, the Giants found themselves down by a run in the ninth inning of Game 7 of the 1962 World Series. With the tying run on third and with the winning run on first, Willie McCovey stepped to the plate and hit a screaming low liner off Yankee pitcher Ralph Terry. It looked headed for the right-center field gap. This would give the Giants the series. At the last moment, second baseman Bobby Richardson snagged McCovey's shot giving, the New Yorkers the series.

A game for the ages occurred on July 2, 1963, when two future Hall of Famers were pitted against each other in Candlestick Park. Before a crowd of 15, 921, a twenty-five-year-old Juan Marichal of the Giants took on Milwaukee's ace Warren Spahn. Marichal was 13–3 at that point, and Spahn was 11–4. They were scoreless after nine innings, and Giants manager Alvin Dark asked Marichal if he wanted to go back to the mound to pitch the tenth. Marichal responded by pointing out that Spahn was continuing to pitch—and Spahn was forty-two years old! As he told Dark, if Spahn was forty-two and he was twenty-five, he had to keep pitching. So they did! It was scoreless until one out in the bottom of the sixteenth, when Willie Mays hit a solo homer to left for the walk-off win. After four hours and ten minutes, it was finally over. Both pitchers were still in the game. That night Marichal gave up only

eight hits in sixteen innings. Spahn yielded only the one run on nine hits in fifteen and one-third innings.

"Hitting is timing. Pitching is upsetting timing."
—Warren Spahn

On a Thursday night in Los Angeles, in September 1965, Sandy Koufax threw a perfect game. The Dodgers got him only one run on one hit. Koufax struck out 14. The amazing part was who he faced. The Cubs were a poor team in the sixties, but the beef in the middle was three Hall of Famers named Billy Williams, Ron Santo, and Ernie Banks. Together they would hit nearly 1,300 career home runs. To get the final out, Koufax needed to get out Harvey Kuenn, a former AL batting champ. Koufax struck him out!

Within thirty days another great game of the sixties occurred in Minnesota, during the World Series. The Dodgers and Twins had won three games apiece going into the seventh game. Unsure until almost game time, Walt Alston, the Dodger manager, went with the lefty Koufax on two days' rest rather than Don Drysdale. Drysdale would be warming up in the LA bullpen from the opening pitch if Koufax faltered. Koufax, who had two pitches, a curveball and a moving fastball, walked Oliva and Killebrew in the bottom of the first to get into trouble. He got out of the inning but knew he could only get the fastball over for strikes. So did the Twins. Minnesota's loaded lineup included MVP Versalles, Oliva, Killebrew, Allison, Mincher, and Battey, and they waited knowing every pitch was to be a fastball. At the end Koufax pitched a shutout, struck out 10, and gave up 3 hits. The Dodgers won the world championship by a score of 2–0.

On October 1, 1967, the impossible dream became a Boston reality. That day the Sox were down 2-0 in the sixth against the Twin's twenty-game winner, Dean Chance. With two on, Carl Yastrzemski unloaded and tied the game 2–2. The Red Sox would go on to win 5–3 to capture the pennant. With the whole season on the line, how did Yaz do under the pressure? He went 4 for 4 with 2 RBI and a run.

One can argue which games of the decade were the best. Certainly Game 7 of the 1964 World Series, with a worn-out Bob Gibson ending the Yankee dynasty that had existed since the 1920s with a 7–5 victory, rates right up there. How about the final game of the 1969 World Series, which made the Mets "amazing"?

Even the 1964 All Star game rates as one of the best. Going into the bottom of the ninth at Shea Stadium, the American League led the National League by a score of 4–3. Willie Mays started a rally and made it 4–4. Then with two on the Phillies' Johnny Callison hit a three-run walk-off for a 7–4 victory.

The sixties were loaded with great players, and they made great moments and great games!

IMPORTANT TRADES OF THE NATIONAL LEAGUE

There were many trades in the decade. This was a time without free agency, and trades were the main way players went from one team to another. Nonetheless, there seems to be five trades that had major results on the outcome of the 1960s.

The Lou Brock trade by Chicago to an out of contention Cardinal team led to the 1964 world championship. In addition, it would be unlikely that the Birds would have won two more pennants and a 1967 World Series without Brock. The speed and enthusiasm that Brock provided to this team was the difference in the Cardinals' success.

The Frank Robinson trade from Cincinnati to Baltimore without a doubt changed the playing field not only in the American league but in the National League as well. Immediately after becoming an Oriole, Robinson led Baltimore to a 1966 world championship sweep over the Dodgers. Robinson was the AL MVP and won the Triple Crown in 1966, and he had many more great years for the O's and had another seven or eight quality years in front of him—yet the Reds deemed him too old at thirty!

The Robinson trade had a major effect on the National League outcome for the Reds. Pinson seemed lost without his high school buddy. By 1967, Rose was even dropped from his famed leadoff spot to third, to make up for the loss. The Reds went from scoring 825 runs in 1965 (Robinson's last year with the team) to 604 in 1967. The team would never finish the decade higher than third. What would the Reds have done if they had not made the trade? This was a time that they were adding Johnny Bench, Lee May, Tony Perez, and others to a veteran Vada Pinson and a maturing Pete Rose, among other quality players. Would the Orioles have had the success they had, and would the Reds have had a different future? In the history of the game, fewer trades have had the impact that this one had—and fewer trades have had such a ridiculous reason for justification. As bad as it was for the Reds, they were able to make up for much of it in a few years when they would get the oil for the Big Red Machine in a trade for Joe Morgan, but that was not until the seventies.

In the Orlando Cepeda for Ray Sadecki trade in 1966, it seems that the Giants did everything possible to never win a world championship in the sixties—from hitting their opponents over the head with a bat (thus suspending their Hall of Fame pitcher Juan Marichal in the middle of a pennant race), to trading a future batting champion in the form of Matty Alou, to trading future MVP and Hall of Famer Orlando Cepeda. Cepeda had an immediate impact on the Cardinals by hitting over .300 for the rest of the 1966 season. In 1967 he ran away with NL MVP honors, leading "El Birdos" to the world championship over Boston. His leading enthusiasm won Saint Louis another pennant in 1968 before falling just short in seven games to the Tigers for the crown. Ray Sadecki continued to be a journeyman pitching until 1977, with several more teams; his won-loss record with the Giants over four years was a mere 32–39.

Two other trades, which can be lumped into one because they were made for the same season and by the same team, were the Pirates trades involving Dick Stuart and Dick Groat. The slugging Stuart went to Boston for the 1963 season. While licking his chops at the Green Monster in Fenway, he hit 75 home runs, drove in 232 runs, and hit about .270 over the next two seasons for the Sox! The 1960 MVP and batting champ, Dick Groat had hit .294 for the Bucs in 1962. Once with Saint Louis, Groat would be the leading cause for the Cards to reach contention in 1963 and the world championship in 1964. Although the Stuart trade made Boston better, they still were no match for the Yankees. However, the Cardinals benefited greatly from Groat. The Pirates were the big losers here. In 1963 they scored 139 runs less. Bill Mazeroski, normally a seventh- or eighth-place hitter, hit in the fourth spot 62 times and hit fifth 34 times for the season. He rewarded the Pirates by hitting .245 with 8 home runs and 52 RBI in 534 at bats.

The loss of Stuart and Groat, at a time when Pirates still had some of their 1960 team and were adding Willie Stargell and Donn Clendenon to the great Roberto Clemente, resulted in a second-division team for 1963 season, where they would stay most of the remainder of the decade. I wonder what they call the guy in Pittsburgh who traded away the two Dicks?

IMPORTANT TRADES OF THE AMERICAN LEAGUE

Obviously the biggest trade in the American League in the 1960s was Frank Robinson for Milt Pappas, Dick Simpson, and Jack Baldschun on October 9, 1965. It is clearly the biggest trade in all of baseball and changed the power of the National League away from the Cincinnati Reds at a crucial time when they were bringing up a host of young talent. It gave the Orioles exactly what they needed to become the powerhouse of the American League.

As important as this legendary trade was, there were some other trades that had significant impact. The Detroit Tigers improved their club overnight with two trades made within days of each other. In one of the trades they acquired Norm Cash from the Indians for Steve Demeter. In the other trade they got Rocky Colavito from Cleveland for the previous year's batting champ, Harvey Kuenn. These two, matched with Hall of Famer Al Kaline, made the Bengals an overnight wrecking machine on AL pitching.

In April 1960, the Senators traded aging star Roy Sievers to the White Sox for Earl Battey, Don Mincher, and $150,000. Although Sievers still had a couple of power years left, the Washington franchise would leave the next year, and Battey and Mincher would be regular forces for the Minnesota Twins for most of the rest of the decade.

On January 14, 1963, the Chicago White Sox traded future Hall of Famer Luis Aparicio and Al Smith to the Orioles for Ron Hansen, Dave Nicholson, Pete Ward, and future Hall of Famer Hoyt Wilhelm. This was one of those trades that looked good for both sides. Aparicio settled the O's defense while providing excellent speed at the top of the order. In 1966, the year the Birds won the World Series, Aparicio came to the plate an amazing 707 times for them. Coupled with Brooks Robinson, Baltimore's left side of the infield became a fortress. For Chicago, they got needed power from Ward and Nicholson. Hansen filled in nicely at short to replace the traded Aparicio. Wilhelm was excellent in relief and was the needed closer for a good White Sox rotation.

When the Indians reacquired Rocky Colavito for the 1965 season, Cleveland gave up two promising stars. Tommie Agee and Tommy John would leave their mark on baseball for several years to come, whereas Colavito would only have two good seasons before ending his career.

In December 1966, the Cardinals traded third baseman Charlie Smith to New York for Roger Maris. Maris was on the down side of his career; but his impact on the Cardinals with his leadership and clutch hitting would help catapult the Cards to two pennants and a world championship.

TRAGEDIES: A WAY OF LIFE

At the Polo Grounds in the top of the fifth inning, on August 17, 1920, Carl Mays of the New York Yankees hit Ray Chapman in the head with a pitch. The next day Chapman would die of his injuries. In the late 1930s it would be Yankee slugger Lou Gehrig who would be forced early from the game, and he was dead in less than two years from a disease that would take on his name. During World War Two, not only did major league players lose their lives in action, but so did many minor leaguers. During the 1950s, Boston's young new promising first baseman, Harry "The Golden Greek" Agganis, would die at twenty-six of a pulmonary embolism, in his second season. It would be the same decade that Cleveland's phenom pitcher Herb Score would see his career disappear from a line drive to the face, off the bat of Gil McDougald. And it goes on and on, from the death of Roberto Clemente and Thurman Munson in plane crashes to the shooting of Lyman Bostock. Each decade continues to be surprised at the untimely death or the sudden ending of its promising stars. The 1960s were no different.

Flying in a small plane over Provo, Utah, on February 13, 1964, Ken Hubbs, the former rookie of the year of the Chicago Cubs, was killed when the plane went down. He was only twenty-two. At the close of the 1966 World Series, baseball would have to once again absorb another tragic blow as thirty-year-old Sandy Koufax would be forced into retirement because he could no longer survive the pain of his pitching arm. In August 1967, it would be Boston's star Tony Conigliaro who would see his

WALT BOND   of-1st base

career derailed when he was struck in the face by a Jack Hamilton pitch. Conigliaro would later have a heart attack at thirty-nine and remained in a vegetative state until his death at a mere forty-five years old. And in September 1968, former Houston slugger Walt Bond would pass away from leukemia; he was only twenty-nine years old.

So Who Really Were the Best Teams in Baseball in the '60s?

In the sixties, the Baltimore Orioles won more regular season games than any other team in baseball, with 911 wins. The Giants were second in baseball at 902 wins. To declare either the best would be a little naive. The O's won only two pennants and one world title. The Giants won only one pennant, and that was a result of a ninth-inning rally in Game 3 of their postseason playoff against the Dodgers in 1962.

It is hard to argue that the best franchise of the sixties wasn't the New York Yankees. They reeled off five straight pennants and captured two titles from 1960–1964. Despite coming apart at the seams in 1965 for the next several years, at the end of the decade, no one else could claim that many titles.

Because the of Yankees' success and then their debacle, the decade might be better to review in sections, with New York the clear winner in the earlier years of the decade from 1960–1963. The Dodgers, who swept the Yanks in the 1963 World Series, were probably the best franchise from 1963–1965; they won three pennants and two championships before the Orioles swept them in the '66 series. Don't forget that they tied for the pennant in 1962 with the Giants, before barely losing the playoff.

With the Orioles' 1966 World Series sweep over the Dodgers, Baltimore won two pennants and a world title between 1966–1969, and they began to dominate baseball during this time. They would continue their run well into the seventies. They clearly were the best in the last four years of the sixties.

Although the Saint Louis Cardinals would win two world championships and three pennants, they placed fourth behind the Yankees, Dodgers, and Orioles due to their poor showings in their non-title years. The Birds finished seventh, sixth twice, fifth, and fourth in 1969, when in a division of only six teams. They did finish second in 1963, but that was to the Dodgers. It's not to say that Saint Louis didn't have some great years in the 1960s, because they did, but they had several poor ones, too.

Which League Was the "Best"?

When I was twelve years old, I got the chance to go to the 1966 All Star game, held in Saint Louis. It was a game that most remember because of the heat; some estimate that temperatures climbed to as high as 106 degrees that day. Players and fans alike suffered from heat exhaustion. Many were taken out by stretchers to local hospitals. Regardless, the game itself was kind of boring despite going into extra innings. The National League won in the tenth, 2–1, when Maury Wills singled home Tim McCarver with the winning run. However, the thing that I still remember the most was when the National League took the field. The outfielders running out for the top of the first were Hank Aaron, Willie Mays, and Roberto Clemente. The starting pitcher was Sandy Koufax. All of them were immortals of the game. Even at my young age, I knew I was seeing something special.

The point of this was that the American League, despite having many great players, could not match the numerous stars and Hall of Famers that played in the National League in the sixties. The number of people that would go on to Cooperstown and that played in the All Star games during this time frame was remarkable. As a result, the National League won almost every game played.

WHERE'S THE BEEF?

Well by now we know where the beef was, and where it wasn't. The question to answer is this: did it matter? From the early years of Babe Ruth and the Yankees to the present day, teams have been striving to add power to the middle of the lineup. Looking at the top teams of the 1960s, the Yankees had plenty of beef in their years prior to 1965. Our runner-up team, the Dodgers, had very little beef and were forced to manufacture runs; they did, however, have the great pitching. The Orioles, the winningest team of the sixties, were blessed with power in the middle and great pitching. The Cardinals, two-time world champions, were average in the middle but had a strong top of the line up in Lou Brock and Curt Flood, and they combined that talent with good pitching.

The answer to our million-dollar question lies in the San Francisco Giants. No team could compare to their beef. They had three Hall of Famers in the 3-4-5 spots in Mays, McCovey, and Cepeda. In addition they could add the Alous, Jim Ray Hart, Harvey Kuenn, and Manny Mota to the mix when needed. They had a very good pitching staff, including two hurlers that would become Hall of Famers, Juan Marichal and Gaylord Perry. The Giants were the only team to win over 900 games besides the Orioles in the sixties. Yet they barely won one pennant.

If the beef is powerful enough, like some of the teams mentioned above, you will win a lot of ball games, but there is no guarantee to winning pennants. The Dodgers and the Orioles proved that much of the time, outstanding pitching beats outstanding hitting. Although pitching tends to win championships, it's not the reason we turn on ESPN for the highlights. I know that when I was a kid, my favorite teams to watch—besides my coveted Cardinals—were the Giants, Braves, and Yankees. Why? Because they had the beef. Why do we need to have so much beef? It's because that's what America likes. As the saying goes, "Beef—it's what's for dinner!"

About the Book

Since Babe Ruth joined the New York Yankees in the 1920s, America has been intrigued with baseball sluggers and teams that stuff the middle of their batting order with power. Even today, sports fans flip to ESPN to see who hit the dingers of the day. Yes, we like to see great catches and outstanding pitching performances, but it's the home runs we live for. The 1960s was a decade of some of the greatest slugging combinations in baseball history. From Maris and Mantle to McCovey and Mays, the decade's memories will live forever !

About the Author

As a longtime baseball enthusiast and historian, I felt the need to reflect on the baseball world of the 1960s. This is a decade that not only do I cherish, but I had the opportunity to personally enjoy nearly one thousand games. As a fan and as a peanut vendor for several years this gave me the opportunity to see my heros up close. This included many of the greats of the game—people like Willie Mays, Hank Aaron, Stan Musial, and Sandy Koufax, to name a few.

As a native Saint Louisian, I was brought into the Cardinal Nation at a young age. Many of these stars and players from the decade have passed on, and I feel it a necessity to carry on with their contributions and their part of our national pastime. The detail of my research hopefully brings a different perspective of the game as it was some fifty years ago. If you were a kid in the 1960's the personal touch of the times will bring back many of your own personal memories as you relive one of the greatest times in baseball history !

ACKNOWLEDGEMENTS

To my wife , best friend and soul mate…..Laura….Thank you for the constant encouragement and confidence through the entire process. You are special !

To my wonderful daughter… Lindsey ..Thank you for letting me share my enjoyment of the game with you. Thank you for embracing it!

To an all most perfect son …John…Thank you for taking your precious time and getting me through the computer issues and not having to write the book on a piece of slate !

To my brother Frank (Bear)… Thank you for being part of the childhood antics!

To my Grandmother…. Babe…Thank you for raising me and encouraging my education in a home that was illiterate for most of my early youth.

To former MLB umpire…Jerry Crawford…Thank you for your kindness and generosity. Your Hall of Fame career is only surpassed by your talent as a quality individual.

To my good friend…Kent Myers…Thank you so much for your added input that made the times come alive for everyone that remembers the decade.

To my good friend...Paul Carbone..Thank you so much for your suggestions which made the book a little more warm and fuzzy. Just like you !

To the Cardinal Nation.....Thank you for allowing me to have a life that included baseball!